Contents

Conclusion: A Voice Worth Using   **165**

Introduction

Speak Freely: Words Are Not Violence

Be yourself; everyone else is already taken.
—OSCAR WILDE

As a clinical psychologist, it's a classic cliché for me to ask patients, "And how do you feel about that?" I have literally spent thousands of hours listening to clients—encouraging them to express themselves and helping them find the words to translate their interior life into an organized narrative. Until recently, there was nothing controversial about this. But over the past few years, something has changed.

I've practiced in New York City for nearly fifteen years, and while anxiety has always been common among my clients, the nature of that anxiety has taken a new form. People increasingly express fears of saying the wrong thing—not just in politically charged conversations, but in everyday life. A national poll by *The New York Times* and Siena College[1] found that 84 percent of American adults believe that self-censorship due to fear of retaliation is a "very serious" or "somewhat serious" problem. In other words, this isn't an issue confined to one political side—it's a problem across the board.

The fear of "being canceled" is something I never studied in graduate school. Sure, we learned about rejection sensitivity and personality disorders that involve excessive paranoia about being ostracized. But the idea that self-expression regarding common social or political opinions could lead to a real risk of being shunned—by friends, family, or professional circles—would have sounded paranoid just a few years ago. And yet, here we are. I can't even say these clients are "paranoid" or "phobic," because that would imply their fear is irrational. And the truth is that unfortunately, their fears are *not* unfounded. In my practice, I frequently see two types of clients affected by cancel culture:

1. Those who fear being canceled or suffering other forms of reprisal for speech. They feel they must constantly censor themselves to avoid losing relationships, reputations, or careers.
2. Those who actively participate in cancellations. Sometimes, they are not even doing so out of malice or a genuine belief that the whatever or whomever being "canceled" is truly reprehensible. Rather, they may feel obligated to join in because they fear that if they don't, they'll be the next target on the grounds that their "silence is violence."

Ironically, those in the second category often feel just as trapped and lonely as those in the first. I've worked with clients who have completely cut off family members because of a political disagreement. The "going no contact" trend has accelerated, where individuals sever all ties with family over differences that, just a decade ago, might have led to spirited debates but not total estrangement. These same clients often carry deep fears that they, too, might one day accidentally say the wrong thing and be exiled from their own social circles. It's a "live by the sword, die by the sword" mentality, and it's exhausting.

Meanwhile, America is in an epidemic of loneliness. The U.S. Surgeon General has identified loneliness as a public health crisis, linking it to depression, anxiety, and even physical health problems. I don't believe it's a coincidence that as cancel culture and self-censorship rose, so did loneliness—because true connection requires authentic self-expression. People are walking on eggshells, and as a result, they aren't being real with each other. The demand for authenticity has skyrocketed—Google search trends show that the phrase "be authentic" has more than quadrupled in popularity since 2004.[2] But how can people be authentic when they constantly feel like they must perform a socially approved script in order to avoid backlash?

Adding to the problem, public discourse is increasingly stifled by fear of reprisal. A Gallup and Knight Foundation[3] poll found that 65 percent of college students believe their campus climate discourages free speech. The result? People are retreating from conversations that matter. The less we talk, the more groupthink* festers, and the harder it becomes to challenge flawed ideas or develop our own thinking. Suppressing speech doesn't just silence individuals, it also weakens our ability to solve problems as individuals and on a societal level.

Advocates of stricter speech regulations argue that words can hurt or mislead, and their concerns are valid—bullying, hate speech, and misinformation are real issues. But there is a dangerous flip side to restricting speech in the name of "safety": doing so can create crippling fear, discourage meaningful debate, stifle intellectual development, make people intolerant of diverse viewpoints, and evoke unnecessary anxiety or escalations around verbal

---

* Groupthink is unpacked later in this book, and you may already be familiar with the term. But for now, just understand that groupthink is a psychological phenomenon where groups of intelligent, thoughtful people can turn into echo chambers where irrational and disastrous decisions are made due to an overwhelming desire for conformity within the group.

disagreements. While it's true that words can hurt, we must be precise and accurate about the harm that words can and *cannot* cause, such as physical harm (unless the words are a direct incitement to actual violence).

Words Are Not Violence

The distinction between distress over verbal communication and harm caused by physical violence is plainly illustrated by the legal and ethical codes that bind clinical psychologists everywhere: If a patient tells me he is going to cause serious physical harm to himself or others, I am legally obligated to break confidentiality and alert the proper authorities as part of my legal and ethical duty to warn. On the other hand, if a patient tells me he's going to say something terribly unkind to his neighbor, I am legally *prohibited* from breaking confidentiality to disclose this information. It would be an egregious breach of confidentiality if I were to alert others to "protect" his neighbor from the upcoming insult. The difference is obvious: one situation involves *physical harm*, the other does not. Yes, words can sting and bite, but these are only figures of speech. To behave as if words are equivalent to actual violence represents a disconnection from reality and may lead to painful and unnecessary levels of anxiety. Imagine thinking that saying the wrong thing could be akin to accidentally running someone over with your car, or feeling as though hearing the wrong words could end your life.

Despite the clear difference between words and violence, a phrase or perspective often used to justify speech suppression is, "words are violence." While catchy, this tagline is psychotic if taken literally. In psychological terms, "psychotic" refers to a break from reality, and equating words with actual physical violence is precisely that. While words can be violent *metaphorically* (i.e., "His words were a slap in the face"), behaving as if this is *literally true* sets the stage for estrangement and actual violence in response to the "violent words." Ironically, squashing speech to "reduce violence" may have the *opposite* effect. Research repeatedly shows that intergroup dialogue is the best way to reduce conflict.[4] This holds even in the context of hateful speech, as evidenced by countless reformed agents of hate. For example, Jesse Morton (formerly Younus Abdullah Muhammad), a former Jihadist recruiter for Al-Qaeda turned counter-extremism advocate, says of his work in deradicalizing extremists, "Establishing a dialogue . . . is crucial."[5]

Moreover, the concept that "words are violence" can degrade the gravity of the *actual* violence suffered by victims of domestic abuse, assault and battery, or murder. When people genuinely believe the misinformation that "words are violence," the Latin logic principle, "*ex falso, quodlibet*" (from a false premise, absurd conclusions can arise) applies. The faulty basis that words are violence leads to the perception that hearing an offensive statement makes the listener "unsafe" from something that is physically dangerous, and the initial flawed premise can make people feel justified in extreme responses that they view as reciprocal, sometimes even including responding to the words with *actual* violence.

Humans have an innate affinity for reciprocity, including in response to violence as it pertains to our justice system. Tampering with the meaning of the word "violence" can have a disorganizing effect upon our otherwise socially adaptive sense of reciprocal justice. Reciprocity is a foundational human instinct that fosters cooperation and fairness. Ancient legal systems—such as the Code of Hammurabi, the Qur'an, Judeo-Christian biblical law, and early Roman law—codified proportional justice through principles like "an eye for an eye." These laws were not about promoting vengeance, but rather about ensuring a balanced system of justice that prevented excessive retaliation as well as unchecked predatory behavior. As society evolved, so did interpretations of reciprocity: In modern legal systems, self-defense laws maintain this principle by allowing proportional responses to neutralize threats of physical harm. However, when we expand the definition of "violence" to include words, we distort this ancient framework and open the door to justifying physical retaliation against disfavored or offensive speech.

> *"Words are animals, alive with a will of their own."*
> —Carl Jung (likely, exact origin unknown)

To avoid the disorganizing effects of conflating offensive speech and physical harm, we must respect the boundaries of reality and of current as well as ancient laws around speech and violence. When these constructs become interchangeable, violence feels like a justifiable response to "hate speech," or simply *speech that we hate*. In fact, a 2017 Brookings Institute poll[6] found that nearly 20 percent of college students felt that violence was an acceptable strategy to shut down a speaker. Unfortunately, reality reflects the results of this poll. Here are some recent, real-world consequences of speech being treated as a violent act in the United States, leading to speakers, journalists, and their audiences being physically attacked, intimidated, or violently silenced:

- Riley Gaines (San Francisco State University, April 2023)—Former NCAA swimmer Riley Gaines, who advocates for fairness in women's sports, faced an onslaught of yelling, stomping, and shouting from protesters attempting to drown out her speech. After her event, she was trapped in a room for nearly three hours, even after police arrived, as demonstrators flickered the lights on and off to disorient her and shouted slurs at her. Some in the crowd demanded ransom money in exchange for allowing her to leave safely. What began as a protest escalated into outright coercion and intimidation, as well as depriving

Gaines of her freedom of movement and her right to speak. The event demonstrates how equating speech with physical harm can lead to physical acts of aggression and suppression.

- Michael Knowles (University of Missouri–Kansas City, April 2019 & University of Pittsburgh, April 2023)— At an event at the University of Missouri–Kansas City, Knowles was physically attacked by a masked protester who sprayed an unknown liquid at him, which was initially feared to be bleach but was later determined to be nontoxic. It appeared that the attack was designed to make Knowles think he was suffering a chemical attack, while insulating the attacker from felony charges since the substance wasn't *actually* bleach. The attack occurred during his speech, which was derailed as police dealt with the attacker and investigated the substance (Knowles ultimately persevered and finished his speech). In April 2023, a scheduled debate featuring Mr. Knowles at the University of Pittsburgh spiraled into violent chaos as protesters burned an effigy of him and launched incendiary devices, including fireworks and smoke bombs, into the crowd and at police officers. The violence resulted in a police officer suffering a spinal injury as well as burns and hearing loss; there were also significant damages to police equipment. These incidents illustrate how treating speech as "violence" can embolden individuals to resort to dangerous, unlawful acts of physical violence and intimidation in a "self-defense" response to stop the supposed "attack" of speech they dislike.

- Andy Ngo (Portland, June 2019 & May 2021)—Journalist Andy Ngo, known for his critical reporting on Antifa, was brutally beaten by masked members of the movement in June 2019 while documenting a protest in Portland,

Oregon. The attack left him with a brain hemorrhage, a stark reminder of the violent consequences of attempting to silence journalists through force. Two years later, in May 2021, Ngo was once again recognized, chased, and assaulted by Antifa members, forcing him to seek refuge in a hotel. Even after escaping into the building, his attackers attempted to breach the entrance and called for him to come outside. Police and medics had to escort him from the scene, and he was later treated at the emergency room for a burst blood vessel in his right eye. These repeated attacks on Ngo were apparently driven by a desire to intimidate him from speaking, or by the belief that an attack against him was a "defense" against the "violence" of his journalism—an ideology that justified responding with real, physical violence.

- Berkeley Free Speech Riot (February 2017)—A scheduled free speech event at UC Berkeley was met with outright rioting as masked demonstrators, including members of By Any Means Necessary (BAMN) and Antifa, launched violent attacks against the event and its attendees with the goal of shutting the event down. Unfortunately, they succeeded. Rioters threw Molotov cocktails at police officers and attendees, and physically assaulted individuals they believed to be right-wing supporters. They wielded flagpoles as weapons along with sticks, rocks, mace, and fireworks. A community college professor affiliated with "anti-fascism" activism was arrested and later agreed to a plea deal for charges involving beating attendees on the head with a bike lock. Shortly after, UC Berkeley's *The Daily Californian* ran a headline, "Violence as Self Defense."[7] The rioters' extreme response to a speaking event and the student newspaper's normalization of it highlights how falsely framing speech as a physical threat can be used to justify destructive, violent behavior.

- Kellie-Jay Keen (a.k.a. Posie Parker) Incidents (Tacoma & New York City, 2022)—Kellie-Jay Keen, a British women's rights activist, has been met with violence and intimidation at multiple speaking events in the United States.* In Tacoma, Washington (October 2022), trans activists disrupted a rally for Ms. Keen's "Let Women Speak" tour, where violence and intimidation escalated to the point where the event had to end earlier than planned. Ironically, the women were silenced at the "Let Women Speak" event. The following month, at Keen's "Let Women Speak" event in New York City (November 2022), trans rights activists antagonized and assaulted police and female attendees, forcing the NYPD to arrest nine counterprotesters. Kellie-Jay Keen was unable to even attend this event, as NYPD informed her in advance that they would likely be unable to protect her. Attendees at the event reported feeling physically threatened and harassed by activists who sought to shut down the discussion through force. Trans activists carried flags for "Antifascists Action," a militant so-called** anti-fascist organization.

Each of these incidents serves as a cautionary tale about what happens when people confuse words or ideas with violence—they become more likely to use actual violence in response to the

---

* She has been met with violence and intimidation in other countries, but this book is focused on the United States.

** I'm emphasizing "so-called" here because, like Antifa, this group or movement proclaims itself to be anti-fascist yet its members frequently use violence and intimidation to limit individual liberties such as freedom of expression. In other words, the groups seem to be like a calorie-rich chocolate cake that is mislabeled as a "weight loss food." Just because it is labeled or titled as such doesn't mean the label is accurate.

perceived "assault" of words reflecting ideas they oppose. Rather than preventing harm and promoting safety, this mindset creates real danger, suppresses freedom of expression, and fosters an environment where intimidation replaces dialogue.

Why Do So Many of the Examples Involve Universities?

You may notice that many of the stories in this book involve universities. That's not because concerns about free speech or self-censorship are limited to higher education. Rather, it's because universities have become a powerful starting point for cultural and psychological patterns that ripple through nearly every other domain—workplaces, families, research, and media. What starts on campus rarely stays there. What begins as an academic preference can evolve into a social script—and eventually, a professional expectation.

Universities play an outsized role in shaping norms. They help define which opinions are acceptable, what language is permitted, and how disagreement is interpreted. This influence stems not only from the students they train, but from the research they produce and the authority they hold as institutions of knowledge. Many of my clients, even long after graduation, continue to carry assumptions and anxieties that trace back to their university experience. The emotional residue of campus norms shows up in therapy sessions, office politics, and even family dynamics.

Universities shape social norms not only because they educate future leaders and produce influential research, but because they model what kind of speech is considered acceptable. Ideological homogeneity within a power structure can create the impression that dissent is unwelcome and wrongheaded. Political scientist Samuel J. Abrams analyzed national faculty data and found that the ratio of liberal to conservative professors at four-year colleges is about 6:1 nationwide—and in New England, where half of the

Ivies are located,* it jumps to 28:1.[8] In such monolithic environments, students may absorb the idea that ideological alignment is a prerequisite for inclusion in erudite circles. In other words, students steeped in these norms may leave college believing it's not only acceptable but intellectually virtuous to ostracize those who think (and therefore speak) differently.

This narrowing of political diversity amongst faculty has become more pronounced with time. For example, a 2005 study found that the Democrat-to-Republican ratio among psychology professors was 11:1,[9] and by 2016 that number had jumped to 17:1.[10] With numbers like these, it isn't unusual for a school's entire faculty of certain subjects to shape the social and professional assumptions students absorb, particularly when adherence to the uniformity is framed as moral clarity (as the "social justice" framework frequently espoused within the liberal ideology[11] often implies). The more pronounced the faculty skew becomes, the harder it is for students to speak up when practically all of the authority figures are singing from the same music sheet.

Students quickly learn to tailor their ideas to match the values of their professors. In classroom hierarchies, the teacher's perspective carries significant weight—they are the authority of the classroom structure, as well as the subject matter expert and the gatekeeper to high grades and letters of recommendation that function as a passport to professional success. Students know that providing term papers or classroom participation that express agreement with the professor's viewpoint is more likely to resonate with the professor's subjective sense of their contribution

---

* Harvard, Yale, Brown, and Dartmouth are in Massachusetts, Connecticut, Rhode Island, and New Hampshire respectively, and the other half of the Ivies (Princeton, Columbia, University of Pennsylvania, and Cornell) are nearby in New York, New Jersey, and Pennsylvania. This means that one of the most elite constellations of universities in the world are likely some of the most ideologically homogenous.

overall and will likely affect their grade.[12] This becomes a compounding problem, because the more that students with diverse viewpoints feel intimidated to express themselves in the classroom, the more an illusion of unanimity is created around the teacher's viewpoints, and the more difficult it becomes to "buck the trend" and speak up.* These conditions within the intellectual environment facilitate *groupthink,* which is unpacked further in chapter 3.

These patterns don't end at graduation. University culture often becomes workplace culture. Human resources departments look to higher education and the research it produces when designing organizational policies on diversity, equity, and inclusion (DEI) and other topics that involve the social sciences. As a clinical psychologist, I quietly cringe when I hear well-intentioned people quoting "the latest research" as if it's gospel. Having worked in quite a few psychology labs, I've observed the pronounced liberal bias that underlies this research firsthand. This partiality has also been documented in scholarly journals in terms of the types of papers that are accepted for publication.[13] I've seen clients silenced

---

* A powerful demonstration of the potential compounding effects of silence begetting more silence is shown in the trends of polls by the Knight Foundation. While their 2016 poll found that 73 percent of college students felt their free speech rights were secure on campus, that number plummeted to 59 percent by 2020, and sank even lower to 43 percent by 2024. This trend is likely due to a variety of factors, but many people find it difficult to be the lone voice speaking up against an increasingly homogenous front, especially in the power dynamic of a student challenging a professor.

Knight Foundation and Ipsos, *College Student Views on Free Expression and Campus Speech 2024: A Look at Key Trends in Student Speech Views Since 2016* (Miami, FL: Knight Foundation, 2024), https://knightfoundation.org/wp-content/uploads/2024/07/Knight-Fdn_Free-Expression_2024_072424_FINAL-1.pdf.

Gallup and Knight Foundation, *First Amendment on Campus 2020 Report: College Students' Views of Free Expression* (Washington, DC: Gallup, Inc., 2020), https://knightfoundation.org/wp-content/uploads/2020/05/First-Amendment-on-Campus-2020.pdf.

at work for expressing views outside the progressive mainstream on topics like abortion, immigration, or gender and sexuality due to a carefully researched corporate stance about "best practices." Some felt their viewpoints had to be hidden, or they'd be quietly excluded from professional or social events. In one case, a client referred to it as being "uninvited to the barbecue"—a metaphor for social ostracism that felt all too real.

So, yes, there are a lot of academic examples in this book due to the unique dynamics and influence of universities, But my experience as a psychologist tells me that even if you're no longer a student, you can still find these university-based examples relatable based on your past academic experiences, the experiences you've observed through friends or family who attend or work at academic institutions, your experiences in the workplace and beyond, or simply by watching the news or encountering research that derives from these hotbeds of "thought leadership." Recognizing the current university dynamics is not an attack on higher education. It's an opportunity to see clearly as we seek to restore open dialogue for the sake of mental health and intellectual progress.

Is This a Democrat versus Republican Issue?

Just to address an elephant in the room: You might notice that the examples above, whether about conservative voices being silenced in academia or through political violence or other related issues, mostly involve left-wing, progressive, or liberal academics and activists using hard or soft power, discrimination, violence, or other forms of intimidation to interfere with the speech of people or groups that are affiliated with more conservative positions. This is not to suggest that these tactics are wrong only when used by the Left. The reason this selection of events is skewed to the left is because in our current landscape, this type of activity simply seems to be occurring more frequently within the Left, and I was unable to locate a significant pattern of contemporary attempts by individuals on the Right to suppress the speech of those on the Left. I sincerely wanted to do this, because I was concerned about this book becoming unnecessarily politically divisive, but was unable to do so.

Similarly, but on a much milder scale of social hostility, there is an observable pattern of social exclusion by the left to the Right but not in the reverse: Liberals are statistically much more likely than conservatives to respond to political differences by defriending on social media[14] or in real life;[15] declining to date;[16] disinviting or shouting down[17] a speaker; decreasing time with family members;[18] or even dropping family members by cutting them off completely.[19, 20] This pattern arises later in this book, and for the sake of brevity it will be described as "the five Ds" (defriending, divorcing, declining, disinviting, decreasing, dropping). People who decline, reduce, or end relationships over politics typically cite very good reasons for their exclusionary behaviors: If they exclude someone for political reasons, they often use labels like "Nazi," "fascist," "genocidal," "misogynist" "transphobic" or "racist" to explain their decision. A recent poll found that 78 percent of Democrats feel the Republican Party has been taken over by racists.[21] Presuming agreement with these labels, the exclusionary behaviors are quite reasonable.

For balance, it's noteworthy that conservatives absolutely have been staunch advocates for limits on free speech in the not-so-distant past, with liberals playing the opposite role. For example, conservatives led the "war on obscenity" in the 1960s–1980s (when conservative groups tried to ban pornography, and George Carlin was arrested for swearing). Conservatives spearheaded efforts to ban "indecent music" in the 1980s–1990s through groups like Parents Music Resource Center, led by conservative figures like Tipper Gore. Indeed, conservatives have *often* been on the side of censorship in the past, and liberals (as the name implies) have often advocated for wider limits on freedom of expression. The current dynamics are actually quite novel. So please understand that this book is not here to pigeonhole either party as the "free speech bad guy." I just wanted to acknowledge that this book's menu of current examples of calls for censorship, and those calls' conflation of words with violence, happen to skew to the left—and this is simply because that's where the vast majority of current examples happen to originate. Even if you disagree with this characterization, please be assured that "left or right" issues are actually tangential to the point of this book, which is simply to highlight the benefits of free speech and share techniques to unlock them. No matter who is trying to quash speech, even with the best of intentions, there can be inadvertent and problematic consequences to our mental functioning.

More than Politics

This book explores why defending free speech is not just a political issue—it's also a mental health issue. Stifling speech stifles people. Self-censorship can lead to emotional repression, isolation, and intellectual stagnation—all of which make us less connected, less resilient, and less capable of solving problems as individuals and as a society. In a culture that increasingly rewards conformity, we must examine the psychological, social, and political consequences of silencing diverse voices; and embrace the *benefits* of freedom of expression. Free speech protects all of us—not just from the state, but from intellectual and emotional stagnation.

Free speech helps to:

- Support our best cognitive and emotional functioning,
- Facilitate strong social bonds, and
- Set the stage for human flourishing.

Yes, words can hurt, but we are built to withstand hurt, and to grow from challenging experiences. We must be antifragile.

Moreover, accepting the idea that others' words can threaten our existence or the existence of others is ultimately undercutting our own resilience as well as our respect for others. We can choose to limit our exposure to voices we find aren't worth our time, but this is completely different from attempting to silence those voices from speaking at all by advocating for their speech to be categorized as illegal, or at least, prohibited from the public square.* This book will help you to understand the cognitive, emotional, and social benefits of free speech, and teach you how to unlock those benefits in your everyday life.

---

* Obvious exceptions include speech that is slanderous, libelous, clearly incites violence, or other forms of speech that are already illegal. This is unpacked further in item 2 in chapter 4, Common Objections to Free Speech.

PART ONE

Chapter 1

The Cognitive Gifts of Language

The word is a powerful lord . . . it can stop fear and banish grief and create joy and nurture pity.
—PLATO

Language is such a basic part of life that many of us rarely stop to consider what an exquisite and powerful tool it is. Evolutionary psychologists, for example, have speculated that the gift of language was essential to humans developing such sophisticated societies. Our robust capacity for complex language allows us to rapidly exchange information, establish trust, form social bonds, enjoy humor, negotiate compromises, create future plans, work collaboratively and innovatively, and pass knowledge through generations.

Naturally, language touches us both cognitively and emotionally. To fully comprehend the stunting effect of stymieing our gift of language through the stifling of speech, we first need to understand the role of language in these two essential domains of human functioning. This chapter will explore the cognitive gifts of language—how language helps us think, problem-solve, gain insight, and regulate our mental processes. In the next chapter,

3

we'll turn to the emotional gifts of language—how it helps us process feelings, build emotional resilience, and foster deep human connection.

Throughout this and the next chapter, I'll clarify distinctions among various therapeutic and academic approaches to the role of language in cognition and emotion. This serves two purposes: First, to avoid making sweeping generalizations about how psychology understands mental processes, since there are variations across different schools of thought. Second, to show that despite these differences, a common conclusion emerges: Language is essential to achieving and sustaining optimal mental functioning—and the richer our linguistic toolset, the better.

> *"To restore language to a person is also to restore a person to the world."*
> —Oliver Sacks (from his work with patients suffering neurological conditions, reflecting the link between language, identity, and mental integration)

Four Core Cognitive Benefits of Language

The cognitive benefits of language are not just abstract—they are measurable and impactful, influencing how we process information, solve problems, and refine our understanding of the world. We have specific regions of the brain that are dedicated to the production of speech as well as comprehension of speech,* suggesting that language is a primal part of our existence, essential to our survival. Human language is uniquely defined by syntax, symbolism, generativity, and the ability to express abstract or imaginary concepts. As we unpack the key cognitive benefits of language in the section below, you may notice some overlap

---

* Broca's area in the left frontal lobe and Wernike's area, respectively.

between the details in the explanations of each benefit, and some of the benefits also appear in the "Emotional Gifts of Language" chapter that follows. This is because the benefits aren't entirely discrete; they are interrelated facets of the incredible gift of language. For example:

- Written language helps with problem-solving.
- Collaborative discussion also helps with problem-solving *and* helps with social support.
- Social support helps with emotional resilience, which in turn bolsters our ability to face problems.

While there is certainly overlap between these benefits, and one benefit often facilitates the other, we'll take a moment to spotlight each of the important features of language. I want you to understand the amazing role that language plays in cognitive processes and understand the potential harms of disrupting these essential processes through restrictive speech codes, whether those codes are formal or implied. As you can see from the circular pattern of the benefits listed above, blocking one spoke of the "communication wheel" could cause problems all around.

Here are four of the greatest cognitive gifts of language:

1.   A Fundamental Process to Organize and Label Our Interior Life

Inside the mind of an intelligent, active person, countless semi-formed, incomplete thought streams can swirl at any given moment. When we choose to bring our interior life into the external by speaking or writing, we are forced to organize these thoughts by selecting one idea—in fact, one word at a time—to express ourselves. Whether speaking or writing, we are compelled to:

- Prioritize ideas based on relevance or importance.

- Streamline chaotic thoughts into coherent sentences.
- Label emotions and concepts with precision, transforming abstract experiences into specific and concrete language.
- Conform to the rules and syntax of language, thereby creating a basic social bond with others who speak our language.

This organization isn't just helpful—it's neurologically significant. Research shows that labeling emotions can actually reduce activity in the amygdala, the region of the brain that becomes activated when we are fearful.[1] By organizing abstract internal experiences into the systems of semantics and syntax inherent to human language, our brain "settles down." We gain control over our thoughts, and we can think more rationally, improving our decisional capacities and increasing our chances of forging alliances that can be helpful to our survival or chances of reproduction. Moreover, in addition to the previously mentioned presence of neural regions that appear to be devoted to the production and comprehension of speech, scientists have discovered that humans have a unique version of the FOXP2 gene, which has been nicknamed "the language gene." Mutations to this gene are linked to severe speech and language disorders. Even infants show preferential brain activation at the sound of human voices compared to other sounds.[2] All this underscores how essential the process of language is to our basic functioning.

Most modern psycholinguists agree that the process between language and cognition is bidirectional, meaning that we use language to *express* our thoughts, and the language we happen to speak can also *shape* our thoughts. This suggests language plays an even more profound role in our ability to organize and label our thoughts and to bridge the gap between ourselves and the external world. It means that stifling our ability to use language freely could have an even more stunting effect upon our cognitive processes than if language merely expresses our thoughts on a one-way street from the brain to the mouth. If learning language and broadening our vocabulary helps us to express ourselves, then when we are forced to "disappear" certain words as they become verboten, the functional loss might be (on a much grander scale) akin to removing a key feature of one of the most frequently used apps on your phone—it limits your ability to use your phone in the full, facile manner that you did before the feature was removed. In this analogy, your brain is the phone and the "key feature of your frequently used app" represents any word or viewpoints that you feel you're "not allowed" to use, especially when they represent ideas that are important to you. A person choosing to limit their own language of their own free volition is not necessarily stifling themselves—as long as the thinker and speaker are in control of their faculties, whatever words they choose to omit are ultimately part of their own expressive choices. But when words and/or viewpoints are dictated as "removed" to them by some external force, a stunting effect would seem inevitable. There is also a gray area where speech isn't legally verboten, but strong institutional pressure makes speaking up extremely difficult. When we habitually suppress our speech to conform to these types of requirements, we can eventually lose touch with our awareness and autonomy around the choice. This is unpacked further in the "Hidden Dangers of Self-Censorship" chapter.

In addition to the cognitive theory of language above, it's also noteworthy that in psychoanalytic psychology, where the mind is basically divided into the conscious and unconscious (there's also the preconscious, but we can put that aside for this discussion), the unconscious is defined as being preverbal. This is partly why much of psychotherapy often involves making a concerted effort to "dive deep" into the "back of our head" and examine what unconscious assumptions or beliefs we may hold, so that we can understand how they may influence our conscious life (and then

work on restructuring them if we realize, upon conscious examination, that they are flawed or maladaptive). This "bringing forth"
of the unconscious is done by working to put the unconscious
experiences into language so that we can better evaluate it. In
other words, putting our unconscious life into language is one of
the first steps in addressing it.

When we prevent the conscious mind from dealing with
material that is ready to emerge from the unconscious—or when
we deliberately "stuff down" material from the conscious into the
unconscious because it's uncomfortable to address—we interrupt
not only our cognitive awareness and our ability to make wise
choices based on that awareness, but also our ability to process the emotions associated with the material. This disruption
can occur either because we lack the linguistic tools to bridge
the unconscious into the conscious mind, or because although
we have the tools, we avoid using them when the material feels
too overwhelming or taboo. The problem is explored further in
chapter 3, "The Hidden Dangers of Self-Censorship," in terms of
suppression, repression, denial, and acting out.

A final point on the basic, fundamental role that language
plays in organizing an otherwise largely chaotic interior life is to
consider that occasionally, different parts of the brain are used
for different types of linguistic expression. Specifically, a different part of the brain becomes activated when we swear or curse
than when we use everyday language. In fact, it's not uncommon
for people who have suffered aphasia (loss of language) following
brain injuries to still be able to curse even though the rest of
their language abilities are lost. I'm not aware of any studies to
confirm either way, but I would be curious if we might see a similar pattern when we dare to use "politically incorrect" language
or have conversations about topics we know some may view as
"wrong" to discuss (or that have been "banned" in the public
square). Either way, what we do know is that being prohibited

to use certain words can, effectively, limit your ability to fully use your brain since certain categories of words have unique patterns of neural activation.

2. Enhancing Problem-Solving Abilities

Translating an amorphous internal experience into a system of language makes it easier to solve problems, particularly complex ones. Being able to "put our thoughts on the table" helps us to examine them, share them with others, and consider different ways to connect the information we have—like putting puzzle pieces on a table and taking time to ponder the way they fit together.

When we use our gift for language to engage in dialogue with others about complex problems, we can:

- **Clarify the issue** by sorting through differences in how we define the problem.
- **Open up new perspectives** through the knowledge and experience verbalized by our collaborators. When we gather helpful information from others, our own bank of resources is enriched. Even if they aren't exactly "collaborators" and may not have any particular knowledge or experience to share, dialogue with others can still be incredibly enriching. Who hasn't benefited from a supportive, intelligent person who makes an excellent "sounding board"?
- **Increase focus:** By having to explain our perspective to others, and then processing their response, we are forced to use additional parts of our brain than if we were pondering the matter in isolation. Bringing more of our brainpower to bear on the matter helps ensure a higher level of focus. We also experience the positive pressure of social norms to appear attentive when the other person is speaking, and to respond with something relevant when they participate

in the dialogue. This is partly why sometimes it's easier for the mind to wander away from productivity when we are working in isolation.*

- **Generate solutions** by building on each other's ideas through dialogue. For example, two friends named Sam and Mara are discussing a short vacation they plan to take together. Mara feels overwhelmed by all the choices; Sam expresses that he'd love to see a few museums but is concerned there won't be enough time. Mara might respond by saying that she loves Sam's idea, and in fact she had a friend who recently mentioned something about a tour bus that could make things easier. Mara promises to follow up with her friend and circle back to Sam. Mara and Sam have both helped the other find a solution to their problem—Mara needed someone to select a goal out of an overwhelming number of options, and Sam needed someone who could think logistically about his particular goal.

- **Increase motivation:** Humans can be motivated by positive social feedback or a desire to enhance our image. Sometimes, showcasing our intelligence and problem-solving skills in collaboration with others can be a way to obtain positive feedback or improve social standing. For example, Sam and Mara may each have derived a sense of pride and enjoyment over their contribution to the vacation plans being well received by each other. This might have partially motivated their contributions in the first place; and the positive feedback they received from one another might motivate them to continue sharing ideas with one another.

---

* Of course, in some situations we may actually focus more intently when we are undisturbed by the chatter of others. However, there are many other situations where an engaged collaborator can help to increase focus on the task at hand.

You probably don't need a scientific study to convince you that "talking things through" with others can help to develop good ideas and solve problems. But just to underscore the point, consider that researchers at the Dresden University of Technology had participants design an everyday object.[3] Participants were then placed by researchers into an experimental condition where they discussed the object by answering questions about it (out of earshot of other participants) or into a control group where they did not have this opportunity. Participants who were guided to discuss their object showed statistically significant differences from the control group. After the discussion period, significantly more participants in the experimental condition "developed new principles and added new explanations of function to their design" than participants in the control condition. Similarly, another group of researchers had one set of participants verbalize their reasons for making moves in a Tower of Hanoi task, compared to a control group that was not given the instruction to verbalize.[4] The verbalizing group significantly outperformed the non-verbalizing group. While there are plenty of studies to show that dialogue can boost problem-solving abilities, the colloquial terms "talk it over" and "talk it through" illustrate this as well—when we talk about challenges, we gain a palpable sense of perspective and control over the topic.

The problem-solving benefits of language are not limited to work we do with others. Language can help us solve problems independently as well, such as by journaling, which has been demonstrated to boost problem-solving skills.[5] Language is also essential to the writing process, of course, and since our working memory can only hold approximately seven items at any given time, the ability to jot down multiple components of a complex situation helps us to navigate multifaceted problems more smoothly. Writing also helps us to encode and process information more deeply, as well as document our thought process or easily review information when we want a refresher.[6] We can use written language to help solve problems while working autonomously, on a whiteboard session in collaboration with others, for episodic collaboration with others over email, or myriad other ways. However we use it, writing is a facet of language that helps us solve problems.

3.   Build Metacognition and Insight

One of the most powerful cognitive benefits of language is that it facilitates our ability to separate our thoughts from our core sense of self. When we speak our thoughts aloud, or write them down on paper, we externalize them, turning them into objects outside of ourselves. This process of detaching from our thoughts and recognizing them as separate from ourselves lets us view them as objects that can be observed and analyzed. cognitive behavioral call this process of thinking about our thoughts metacognition. The process of observing your thoughts and being able to think about them in a calm, rational, language-based manner is also a cornerstone of mindfulness meditation and of cognitive behavioral therapy, which has academically and clinically integrated with mindfulness meditation in recent decades. Mindfulness skills are generally built in mindfulness training or cognitive behavioral therapy by observing your thoughts and then verbalizing them by telling a meditation partner or therapist about your observations, or by writing them in a journal. The goal is, partially, to help you realize that your thoughts are *had* by you, but your thoughts are not *you*. A similar process is found in psychodynamic psychotherapy literature's exposition of the experiencing ego and the observing ego; and this process hinges on language as well:

Psychodynamic literature breaks the ego (for a simplified working definition, in this context the ego might be viewed as one's sense of self) into two parts: the "experiencing ego" and the "observing ego." The experiencing ego is the part that is fully absorbed in whatever is being experienced in the moment, like a baby crying with hunger. The baby is *completely* absorbed in his experience, almost to the point of feeling merged with it; he has no insight about it. The complementary observing ego is the overarching insight that we gain through deeper self-knowledge. For example, an adult who is ravenously hungry doesn't "get lost" within absorption of his experience. He is able to recognize it, label it, and have insight about how his hunger might be shaping his current mood. This insight allows him to make wiser choices (for example, if asked to make an important decision he might respond by explaining he's ravenous and would prefer to address the decision once he's had a meal and can think more clearly). A goal of psychodynamic psychotherapy is often to help strengthen the observing ego.

You may notice something in common from the approaches described above: While they may use different vocabulary, one of the shared goals of psychodynamic psychotherapy, mindfulness meditation, and cognitive behavioral therapy is typically to boost metacognition. Whether by "strengthening the observing ego" or "building mindful awareness," or "learning to label thoughts and feelings," a major objective is often to help people to think *about* their thoughts and experiences objectively. The idea is to give them a "bird's-eye view" of what's happening in their mind. Why would all these disciplines be so focused on this goal? Because building metacognition helps us to:

- Challenge assumptions without feeling personally attacked. We realize that our assumptions are just thoughts we've had, not *parts of ourselves*. We see that thoughts are malleable, and that we can refine or discard them as needed.
- Deepen our thought process. Putting our thoughts into a system of language and evaluating them objectively to make it easier to build on good ideas, use critical thinking

skills, and connect our current thoughts to our previous body of knowledge. Psychologists call this process "cognitive elaboration."

- Practice better self-care. Insight about ourselves empowers us to practice better self-care, such as the previous example about a person who has insight that his hunger is distracting him to the point where he should refrain from important decisions till he's had a meal.

- Have better relationships. When we can explain to others what we're thinking and how we're feeling, it's easier for them to empathize with us, collaborate with us, and build closeness. For example, if the man in the situation above were about to step into an important meeting when he suddenly realized he was ravenous because he hadn't eaten all day, he could quickly and quietly survey his colleagues to see if anyone had a protein bar or some other "emergency snack." This would not only help solve his problem, but could also strengthen his relationships due to the Benjamin Franklin and Pratfall effects,[7] which involve small favors improving relationships (unless he was known for constant emergencies—in that case, his colleagues might tire of his frantic requests). Language facilitates relationships through emotional benefits too; this is explored in other sections of this book. But even on a purely cognitive level, relationships are formed and strengthened by our ability to exchange factual information for purposes of cooperation and collaboration.

- Monitor our thought process. When we can observe our thoughts in a rational, language-based manner, we can enjoy an "early warning detection system" to notice when we're starting to veer off the path of progress. For example, a person who wants to quit smoking might monitor their thought process for what they've noticed are "pre-smoking thoughts" such as "I wonder if anyone here has a cigarette," and do an immediate mental review of a previously created list of their top five reasons for smoking cessation whenever they recognize pre-smoking thoughts arising in their internal monologue.

For a more extensive discussion of mindfulness, metacognition, and their overlap, as well as specific techniques to build mindfulness skills, see my previous book, *Nervous Energy: Harness the Power of Your Anxiety*, where an entire chapter dedicated to this topic. Part 2 of this book also includes many techniques that will peripherally help build mindfulness and metacognition skills through techniques such as journaling, the WAIT test, and narrating your experience, which can guide you to observe yourself without judgment and share those observations with others when appropriate.

4. Reduced Anxiety and Depression

Since we know that language helps organize our thoughts, boosts our metacognition and problem-solving abilities, and improves our capacity for relationships and self-care, it's not surprising that this results in a reduction of anxiety and depression. The features above help to reduce stress, which is a mitigating factor for depression and anxiety. The benefit of reducing depression and anxiety through language is explored later in the book through the lenses of emotion and social support as well, but language is a protective factor for mental wellbeing even on a purely cognitive level. Here are some examples of how this works:

- **Schema therapy:**[8] This type of therapy involves the clinician asking questions that guide clients to discover and articulate their "schema" (essentially their worldviews and beliefs about themselves) and then guiding the client to verbally explore and describe the experiences that led to these beliefs. The therapeutic goal is often to identify maladaptive schemata that are causing the client unnecessary distress. For example, a socially anxious client might have a schema that the world is a harsh place where people will judge you for tiny infractions, and she might discover she developed this schema through a mother who was hypercritical. Once the maladaptive schema and its source are identified, the therapist might introduce cognitive restructuring:

- **Cognitive Restructuring:** This cognitive behavioral technique involves analyzing the thought patterns that arise from maladaptive schemata. People with depression and anxiety often have maladaptive thought patterns that cognitive behavioral therapists locate as the source of their diagnosis. For example, the Negative Cognitive Triad[9] remains a popular cognitive model of depression that conceptualizes depression as a result of negative perceptions about the self, world, and future. In the case of the socially anxious client described above, the therapist might guide the client to list all the supportive people in her life to challenge the client's belief that the world is a harsh place full of judgmental people. Next, the therapist might help the client to develop thought replacements (described below) to use when she finds herself using an old mental "script" (the "script" would be the internal monologue of automatic thoughts that revolve around a world full of harsh, judgmental people).

- **Thought replacements**: Once the maladaptive worldviews and general thought structures are identified, the therapist and client work to identify specific "automatic thoughts" that reflect the maladaptive views ("automatic thoughts" are thoughts that have become so habitual that they occur repeatedly and without examination, at least until intentional effort to do so). Next, the therapist and client craft replacement thoughts for the client to deliberately override the maladaptive thoughts. By deliberately overriding the negative thoughts and dismantling the thought process that leads to excessive anxiety, symptoms of depression and anxiety often resolve; and the new cognitive structure that reflects a revised worldview (or schema) is reinforced. Thought replacements are unpacked in greater detail in my previous book, *Nervous Energy: Harness the Power of Your Anxiety.*[10]

- **Self-Advocacy:** Clients are often guided in therapy to advocate for themselves by gathering information or sharing information with others, with the goal of improving the client's life circumstances. For example, a client struggling with weight gain might be given homework to meet with a nutritionist to learn better dietary habits. A client overwhelmed and overloaded at work might be guided to list all their projects and review them with their boss to understand which items to prioritize. These types of self-advocacy behaviors are so basic to everyday life that we may not realize how much they hinge upon putting our cognition into language and communicating with others to exchange information and help resolve difficulties or get support with challenges.

Conclusion on the Cognitive Gifts of Language

Whether through cognitive behavioral therapy, metacognition, or simply labeling our thoughts and engaging in problem-solving skills, there is ample literature to show that the organizing and communicative aspects of language provide exponential cognitive benefits. Using language helps us to gain control and a sense of objectivity around our cognitive activity, which is often a foundational step in building relationships and solving problems, as well as for psychotherapy to treat clinical anxiety and depression (along with other mental illnesses not discussed here).

When we remove words, topics, or opinions from our "mental menu" of what we can express, we limit our ability to examine that material, reflect on it, or gain insight by discussing it with others. If language is an essential tool for cognitive vitality, then excising parts of our lexicon is akin to removing microscopes, beakers, or other instruments from a scientist's lab: research can still happen, but capacity and precision are impaired.[*],[**] Without labels for ideas or experiences—or when those labels become inaccessible due to legal restrictions or social taboos—it becomes harder to engage with those concepts clearly. This phenomenon is captured by the term *hypocognition*, which refers to the decreased cognitive specificity and interior clarity that results from a limited lexicon. The term was coined by anthropologist Robert I. Levy, who observed that the Tahitian people lacked a word for "grief,"

---

[*]   There is very limited research on the impact of removing language from human cognitive functioning because, on its face, the concept of deliberately creating this situation in a laboratory sounds abusive and unethical. However, limited opportunities for research, often through deaf children who have been unintentionally deprived of exposure to sign language, suggest that language deprivation has negative impacts on comprehending complex ideas and engaging in structured, abstract thought.
       Qi Cheng, Eric Halgren, and Rachel Mayberry, "Effects of Early Language Deprivation: Mapping between Brain and Behavioral Outcomes," in *Proceedings of the 42nd Annual Boston University Conference on Language Development*, ed. Anne B. Bertolini and Maxwell J. Kaplan (Somerville, MA: Cascadilla Press, 2018), 140–152, https://cssh.northeastern.edu/cali/wp-content/uploads/sites/57/2024/09/Cheng-Halgren-Mayberry-BUCLD42-11-1.pdf.

[**] Susan Schaller's book *The Man Without Words* also explores a deaf man who was first exposed to American Sign Language in his late twenties, and documents that acquiring language stimulated new modes of thought for him such as abstract reasoning, greater time awareness, and a stronger sense of self. Susan Schaller, *A Man Without Words*, 1st California paperback printing (Berkeley: University of California Press, 1995).

a linguistic omission he connected to broader cultural patterns of emotional avoidance.[11] As discussed earlier, the linguistic process is bidirectional: researchers collaborating at Stanford and Carnegie Mellon found that verbal labels don't just serve as an outgoing form of communication from the speaker to the world, but the availability of detailed labels actually plays a role in shaping our perception of concepts and categories.[12] Labels help us sort and process information at a granular level; when we are deprived of them, this process is impeded. The dynamics of limiting linguistic expression are explored more fully in chapter 3, "The Hidden Dangers of Self-Censorship."

Vignette: My Personal Last Straw

The rest of the stories shared in this book will be about my clinical work with anonymized (and sometimes amalgamated) stories of clients facing issues related to free speech, but this first story is actually about my own first-hand experience with the issue, and how it led to writing this book.

I moved to Manhattan in 2001, fulfilling a childhood dream. I lived and worked happily there for nearly two decades, building a career as a clinical psychologist, author, and featured expert for various national television shows and other media outlets. The media was an unexpected but much-enjoyed aspect of my work, and it was certainly great for business. There was just one catch: I knew the media generally leaned very heavily toward the left, whereas my own political perspective was more centrist. This didn't have to be a dealbreaker—it just meant that I had to do what I'd done in order to be successful in an Ivy League college and again to earn a doctorate in clinical psychology at a Brooklyn-based university, both of which are environments where the political climate runs staunchly to the left.[13] I laughed at jokes about conservatives that I didn't think were funny to avoid "outing myself," and carefully avoided making any comments that could "blacklist" me in the eyes of professors who had the power to derail my academic progress or journalists who would likely cross me off their go-to list of experts. I never said anything that I felt was untrue, but I sometimes danced carefully to get away from topics where I knew my input would be "problematic." For example, I would comment on issues related to "#MeToo" with sincere condemnation of sexual abusers, but I would refrain from mentioning the very real problem of women who make false allegations of sexual misconduct since it was clear this was not the input being sought.

This strategy worked fine until the COVID-19 pandemic, when I became very troubled by the widespread masking of children, often as young as two or three years old, for multiple hours on an ongoing daily basis. I was extremely concerned about the cognitive, emotional, and social effects this would have upon children, and I was shocked that none of my colleagues were discussing it. As a mother to a then-three-year-old child, I knew I simply couldn't do this to him; yet the only alternative was to keep him in our home in near-isolation all day, since the entire city had mask requirements. We had "treaded water" since the pandemic began in March, but by October I knew we couldn't continue any longer. The weather was getting colder, so even staying at an outdoor playground all day was becoming less feasible. My family and I made the decision to flee to Florida, where we could give our son a normal life. This was a lifesaver for my family, but I was concerned about other kids. I saw parents online discussing their concerns, and I saw them being swatted down by "experts" who belittled them and disregarded their commonsense instinct that it felt wrong to force their children into masks on an indefinite basis. Staying quiet about my concerns as a clinical psychologist was starting to feel more like a moral issue than my past decisions to refrain from public comment on certain topics.

Shortly after moving to Florida, I wrote a piece detailing my concerns about the harms of masking children on a multi-hour, daily basis. It was almost eerie to me that no other psychologists (that I was aware of) were writing about this or discussing it. This made me wonder if I was foolishly missing something embarrassingly obvious about why this was all perfectly fine. I sent the piece to a couple of colleagues and asked them to tell me if there was something inaccurate in what I had written, or if I was missing something that rendered my concerns moot. Their response was shocking to me: They said there was nothing inaccurate and that my concerns seemed valid from a scientific perspective, but that they did not think I should share the piece because it could discourage people from masking their children. Since we knew very well by this point that children were not generally vulnerable to serious harm from COVID-19, a vaccine was available, and my colleagues agreed that my concerns of harm to children were valid, why would they want to discourage me from spreading the word about the potential harms of a "protective" measure that seemed likely to do more harm than good to children? The illogical and irrational quality of my colleagues' reactions was the most profound bump against groupthink I'd ever experienced in a professional setting.

I shared the blog. Going public with my feelings turned out to be quite cathartic, and very well received. For example, my blog was retweeted by Dr. Jay Bhattacharya (now the director of the National Institutes of Health). More importantly, my message helped parents. I received countless messages from parents thanking me for giving them the psychological vocabulary (along with the confidence) to articulate their instinctual concerns and "answer back" at school board meetings, medical offices, and other places where they had been ordered to mask their children all day every day, and to do so without asking questions. They had been told to "trust the science," yet there seemed to be very little actual science driving the directives they received about masking their children. Parents felt gaslit by the "experts," and my blog was giving them at least one small way to re-brighten the lights.

The process reminded me of what I had learned in graduate school about the abuser-victim dynamic where an abuser isolates his victim and undermines her efforts to ask rational questions about their dynamic or seek help. These parents had been shut down on social media and school boards and banned or stigmatized for challenging the mandates. Ironically, to underscore the element of gaslighting, they were often shut down for "misinformation" or told their unwillingness to provide unquestioning cooperation in the masking of their children for days, weeks (and eventually, in many states, years on end) signaled a "lack of compassion." Part of free speech, according to our First Amendment, includes the right to assemble. Gathering together, online or in person, helps groups to find their voice, exchange information, and build solidarity. These parents had felt isolated, and we all noticed that it felt amazing to communicate and discuss the issues openly.

In addition to conversations with parents, I was invited to various TV shows and podcasts to discuss the potential harms of masking children. This was certainly gratifying, but what happened next was striking: by becoming verbal about an issue that I'd previously only pondered in silence, my thought process began to deepen significantly. As discussed in this book, putting thoughts into language is inherently organizing—it forces us to prioritize ideas, streamline chaotic thoughts, and label emotions and concepts clearly.

Discussing my concerns openly allowed me to identify and articulate subtle distinctions that had previously felt vague or fragmented. Talking openly felt like escaping a cognitive and emotional straitjacket created by self-censorship. Open dialogue provided space to elaborate on facets of my views while pruning others through conversations with diverse perspectives.

My thought process around the topic of masking children was becoming more sophisticated, coherent, and comprehensive, and that growth hinged upon the dialogue I was having with others. This transformation in my thinking also mirrors what psychological research shows: when we put emotions into words, we actually calm the brain's fear centers. As I continued to speak openly about this then-controversial topic, I felt a potent sense of emotional relief from the tension that had built up in silence. As my mind relaxed, I could think more clearly and creatively.

The emotional benefits of language, unpacked in the next chapter, were palpable: speaking authentically and receiving a boost of social support helped regulate my emotional intensity and foster resilience in the face of backlash. (Indeed, there was some backlash—but I didn't focus on it much since it was rarely fact-based; more often it was just name-calling by random online trolls. I was too busy engaging in genuine dialogue to be bothered.)

This newfound openness had an expansive effect beyond the initial topic of masking. It felt as though a previously blocked section of my mind had suddenly unlocked, sparking a cascade of thoughts about other taboo or politically sensitive issues. These ideas, once pushed to the edges of my consciousness by fears of ostracization or judgment within my previously homogenous social and professional circles, became available for thoughtful examination. Rather than stifling my own cognitive and emotional processes for the sake of acceptance within media and academic networks, I found that speaking freely catalyzed a richer internal dialogue and strengthened my capacity for authentic self-expression.

Expressing what was meaningful to me as both a mother and psychologist not only brought personal fulfillment but also resonated with others who felt similarly isolated or misunderstood. This shared authenticity and intellectual stimulation prompted me to recognize, for the first time, the inherent mental health benefits of free speech. That insight ultimately led me to research the topic further and, eventually, to write this book exploring and advocating for the importance of free speech and providing others with tools to speak freely and listen resiliently.

Chapter 2

The Emotional Gifts of Language

Once we name it, we can move through it, beyond it.
—BELL HOOKS

Beyond sharpening the mind's cognitive processes, language has a profound effect on our emotional well-being. Speaking and expressing our thoughts is a powerful tool for emotional regulation, self-understanding, and building genuine connections with others.

Countless psychology studies have shown that putting our feelings into words has myriad benefits. In fact, sometimes a stated objective of psychotherapy is to increase the client's emotional vocabulary as a pathway to improving their emotional awareness, ability to connect with others, and capacity for self-care—when we are aware of our feelings and can describe them to others, it's easier to get our needs met.[1]

Before my office went completely virtual, I kept a laminated copy of an emotional vocabulary stimulator (shown on page 26) in my office, and clients struggling to express themselves (often during moments of intense emotion) found it an incredibly helpful tool to "find the words" to articulate their internal experience. Moreover, the mere act of taking an amorphous interior life and putting it into an organized system of language is soothing. Putting our internal experience into language is helpful on a cognitive level, as discussed in the previous section, but it also has a calming effect. It is much like the way that creating order in a disorganized room is helpful not only in terms of utility (like the cognitive benefits of well-organized thoughts) but we also just feel calmer, in-control, and refreshed when our headspace is in an orderly system that is at least basically relatable or explainable to others. In fact, psychodynamic psychotherapists often refer to the process of hearing and understanding a client's experience as

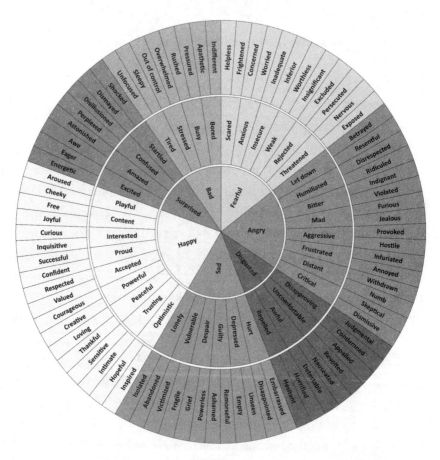

Emotional Vocabulary Stimulator by Geoffrey Roberts

creating a "holding environment"[2] or "containment."[3] This refers to the idea that simply labeling their emotions and feeling understood or "contained" by their therapist helps the client to see their experience as more understandable and manageable— putting their emotional life into words literally makes burdens more relatable, and the client is no longer alone.

The Five Core Emotional Benefits of Language

1. Regulating Emotional Responses

Speaking or writing about our feelings helps to regulate emotional intensity, particularly fear and anxiety. Research has shown that labeling emotions can reduce amygdala activity, making it easier to keep from overreacting and becoming unnecessarily "triggered." The amygdala, sometimes called "the house of fear" in the brain, is highly involved in our reactions to threats. When we perceive danger—like spotting a snake in the grass—the amygdala becomes active. Our automatic, evolutionarily adaptive response is to narrow our mental and even our visual perspective. This mental and physical tunnel vision helps in life-threatening situations but can be problematic in verbal discussions. When an argument triggers the amygdala's alarm bells, we may feel unnecessarily threatened and instinctively react with unwarranted aggression, thereby turning up the heat and escalating the argument.

This response is part of the brain's fight-or-flight mechanism, which prioritizes black-and-white thinking over nuance. In the face of actual danger, such as encountering a surprise rattlesnake, this response is useful—your only concern is avoiding the threat, not seeking to understand the snake's perspective or to preserve your relationship with him. However, when this response is activated in a verbal argument, it can make people behave in a reactionary and confrontational manner that is wholly counterproductive. Instead of fostering discussion, the amygdala hijacks our ability to consider different perspectives, turning complex issues into battlegrounds where the only goal is to "win" rather than to understand.

This is partly why being able to label our feelings can help to diffuse arguments. The person who can pause after being called a racist in the middle of a heated discussion and articulate their internal reaction in an emotionally intelligent way is more likely to build a bridge than someone who responds in kind by escalating with more name-calling or simply shutting down:

> *"I just need to pause for a moment because when you called me 'racist' for opposing race-based affirmative action, I felt misunderstood, ashamed, and even angry at myself for feeling ashamed—I felt all this since I know I'm not racist. I care about you and our relationship, so I want you to know that label feels hurtful to me. You might still see me as a racist, and of course, you have a right to your opinion—but I have a strong visceral reaction against racism, and I think that word is sometimes used to silence people since everyone knows that in this day and age practically nobody wants to be called a racist. I'm not saying that's what you're doing, but I recognize that my first reaction right now is actually to become stand-offish because I've let that label intimidate me in the past and I absolutely refuse to let fear of that inaccurate label silence me any longer. I don't want to get carried away and over-compensate by becoming too aggressive about it though, so I just needed to pause and acknowledge my reaction and explain where I'm coming from before we continue."*

When we take the time to label the feelings that arise when we are *feeling as if* we are "under threat" and connect them to the experiences that led to this sense of threat, we process complex emotions more effectively and adaptively. When we communicate those feelings to others instead of lashing back at them for the supposed threat, we make it easier for them to empathize with us and we reduce escalations.

It may also be helpful to label and communicate positive regard as well whenever appropriate ("I can see we disagree on this topic, but I feel so appreciative that we're able to have an open conversation—thanks for hearing me out and for sharing your own views in such a clear, thoughtful way."). Research shows that expressing authentic positive emotions helps social bonds[4] and can serve as a buffer against stress.[5]

2. Healthy Emotional Detachment and Insight

Just as language helps create cognitive detachment from ideas, it also allows us to develop emotional detachment from our feelings. Similar to the way that externalizing our thoughts facilitates a "birds eye view" of cognitive process (described as metacognition in the previous section), externalizing our emotions by transforming them into language helps us to put them into perspective as well. This organizing process facilitates insight. There's no comparable word to "metacognition" to describe this process, but I would call it "meta-emotion." By speaking about our emotions, we externalize them and make them easier to analyze and process. We can also recognize that our feelings are not our identity; they are temporary experiences that can be examined and understood. This is why a key component of cognitive behavioral therapy (CBT) involves identifying emotions as part of a three-step process:

1. Event (For example, your boss tells you you've made a mistake.)
2. Interpretation (This varies. For some, the interpretation is, "I'm a failure," while for others it might be, "He's always picking on me.")

3. Reaction (Depends on the interpretation, but it might be an emotional response of shame or anger respectively, based on the examples above.)

The reason CBT clients are guided to this three-step process is partly to help them develop a healthy detachment from their feelings rather than feeling fused with their emotional reactions, so they are therefore less likely to become emotionally overwhelmed. Putting our feelings into language lets us trace the precise mental steps that led to them and become more rational about situations where we may have made counterproductive emotional leaps. For example, a person with a fear of rejection might experience intense feelings of abandonment when their loving, stable spouse is running a few minutes late for a date. They can be taught to use the CBT process above to trace the mental leap they're making by taking a harmless event (their spouse is late), interpreting that event a certain way (assuming that their spouse no longer loves them), and then *of course* feeling abandoned based on their catastrophized interpretation.

Revising the interpretation (step 2 in the 3-step CBT process above) is more of a cognitive process, which is discussed in the Cognitive Gifts of Language chapter using an example of a salesperson whose meeting goes poorly. But awareness of the emotion is often what stimulates an examination of the cognitive process. Creating emotional detachment empowers the person to "step outside of themselves" for a moment and prepares them to build a more rational understanding of why they are feeling totally abandoned over something relatively minor and to then revise their interpretation to produce a more appropriate emotional response. Without this process, the person can get stuck wallowing or spiraling into an emotionally reactive response, such as leaving in a huff before their spouse even understands what's happening.

Detachment Also Allows Us to "Trace" Emotions Backward through Bodily Markers of Emotion

A healthy sense of detachment from emotions, rather than feeling merged with them, can help us gain insight through our body-felt sense of emotions as well. Because of emotions' entwinement with our body (we have more serotonin receptors in our gut than our brain, for example), we can also gain emotional insight by paying attention to our bodily signals. Sometimes they provide information before our conscious cognitive mechanisms can fully register the reason why we feel the way we do. This is why sometimes, paying attention to our "gut feelings" can be helpful.

For example, we sense that we don't quite feel calm and secure with someone new in our life. We can't put our finger on why, but we just have a "funny feeling" about them. Without a healthy detachment from emotions, we can "get lost" in this feeling. But if we put it into language and explore it, we can develop insight around it. Oftentimes, exploring this feeling objectively and inviting our mind to offer what psychologists call "free associations" to this person or this feeling (where we just blurt out or write down whatever words, memories, or concepts come to mind when we think of this person or the emotions or physical feelings we have about them, without worrying if the connections make sense), can help to flesh out what underlies the "gut reaction" we've had to the person. Sometimes this exploration of our initial "gut feeling" illuminates a genuine, logical issue of concern about the person, and sometimes it actually reveals that our reaction is illogical and unfounded. For example, you realize you're just responding to them with apprehension because they happen to bear a striking resemblance to a college boyfriend who broke your heart. Once we understand these "funny feelings," we can then bridge them into constructive, rational responses.

Of course, sometimes the process is not interpersonal, and we're just noticing our reactions to the rhythms of our day. We might notice the palpable sense of relief we get at the end of work each day, and it can guide us to consider if we're placing too much pressure on ourselves, or if there's some other workplace dynamic that needs our attention. Either way, the insight we can get from observing our emotions with the sense of curiosity that objective detachment provides can be adaptive. Even on a bodily level, language plays a role in identifying the feeling, sourcing what's driving it, and extrapolating the insight it offers.

Whether by providing a way to objectively trace our emotional responses back to the perceptions and reactions that shaped them, or by strengthening our observing ego's ability to label our emotional experiences and thereby gain a sense of control over them, language plays a crucial role in cultivating healthy emotional detachment. It helps us recognize that our emotional reactions are not permanent parts of our core self, but temporary and ever-changing experiences that we can compare and contrast objectively. Language also facilitates detachment by allowing us to translate our internal life into external expressions that others can understand—inviting empathy, connection, and deeper mutual understanding. In all these ways, language enables us to step back from raw emotion, reflect more clearly on our inner world, and share that world with others in a precise and meaningful way.

3. Building Authentic Connections and Social Support

Social support is so vital to mental health that psychologists are required to assess it during intake evaluations. Previously, this was formalized under Axis IV of the *DSM*'s[6] five-axis system, which included an evaluation of social factors in the patient's life. Even though the *DSM-5* no longer separates diagnoses this way, assessing social support remains essential to any comprehensive psychological evaluation. Strong relationships promote emotional resilience, reduce stress, and aid recovery from mental health challenges. Conversely, loneliness is a known risk factor for depression and anxiety. This is why psychological assessments go beyond symptoms—they examine a person's support system and how it impacts their well-being.

To fully appreciate the importance of social support and the vital role that language plays in it, we need to zoom out and consider humans at their most basic level. Humans everywhere, since known history, have enjoyed the seemingly miraculous gift of language. It appears to be innate. From the moment they are born, babies begin gurgling, then babbling, and eventually they all speak (unless a severe developmental or environmental challenge has occurred). And despite our vastly different languages around the globe, we share similarities: For example, across otherwise disparate languages and cultures, babies all over the world make a sound *something* like "mama" when referring to their mother. Noam Chomsky has posited that a universal grammar encompasses certain basic facets of all language.[7, 8] Language appears to be hardwired into us, almost as if connecting with others is a biological need. This may be why going into solitary confinement is so fearsome to even the most hardened prison inmates, and why we have laws limiting the time a prisoner can be isolated before the punishment would be termed "cruel and unusual."

Psycholinguist Steven Pinker makes the clever comparison that just as a spider needs to spin webs out of an instinctual drive, humans appear to need to talk and connect with one another.[9] This may be why we feel best with friends who let us be ourselves—friends with whom we can have a heart-to-heart, or laugh at jokes that only we understand, and who just seem to "get" us without judgment. Language is at the heart of this type of intimate human connection. When we speak openly and honestly, we foster authentic relationships that are rich with information and based on trust and understanding. This helps us to feel secure—and in fact, we are more secure. On an evolutionary level, we were literally safer when connected to a tribe than navigating the jungle alone. Everyone has different levels of introversion or extroversion, but in general we all need at least some basic level of social connection.

Part of the reason we are hardwired for connection with others appears to be that these connections facilitate cooperation to help get our needs met and further our survival as a species. On the most basic level, for example, we must connect in order to reproduce. Research shows that women in particular release oxytocin during sexual intimacy and during breastfeeding; oxytocin specifically promotes emotional closeness and social bonding. Even outside of this most intimate form of human connection, authentic emotional expression helps us "sync up" with our community and sends signals that help them to meet our needs. This runs so deep, it actually becomes biological even outside of sexual reproduction. We call it reading someone's "body language" when we see their shoulders slumped accompanied by a sad facial expression, because their emotion is permeating their body to the point where it "speaks." Everything from our body language to our tone of voice—as well as, of course, the words we use—are emotional outlets that work in concert to communicate how we're feeling, what we want, and our readiness to connect with others.

The psychobiology of emotional connection is demonstrable on a neurological level as well. For example, "mirror neurons"[10] are specialized brain cells that activate when we have an emotion, and even when we merely observe others having that emotion. This is the neurological underpinning of empathy. In a similar sense, neuropsychologists use the term "neutral coupling"[11] to describe a dynamic synchronization of brain activity that occurs even beyond the mirror neurons; neural coupling is strongest when the listener is paying close attention. When we pair this with the knowledge that specific emotions have unique patterns of overall brain activity[12] as demonstrated by brain imaging tools, we can see that the brain of a person who is listening well actually syncs with the speaker's brain.

The overlap and integration of emotions, body language, and facilitation of interactions with others almost can't be overstated. One of the most profound examples is that when women cry during an argument, a man's testosterone levels naturally and automatically drop; this drop immediately renders him less inclined to be overly aggressive, thereby bolstering the chances of a successful resolution. It's as if Mother Nature has imbued our emotions with socially adaptive functions, and they are ingrained so deeply that they are entwined with our biology. A similar example is laughter, which drops our cortisol. This is partly why humor can be such a lifesaver and bring us together during arguments or stressful moments. These examples illustrate how innate the "syncing" process of emotion is between humans: We need connection, and emotion is a key part of that connection. We literally have complementary chemical and neurological reactions with those around us based upon our shared emotional experience. Language is what helps us to refine and make meaning from those experiences and allows us to convey them to others in a personalized manner that facilitates social bonds.

4. Promoting Emotional Resilience

When we obtain the social support of others, we get what psychologists call "social buffering" that helps to mitigate the effects of stress. This means that with the support of a social network, our problems feel less overwhelming. The ability to speak openly helps individuals build emotional resilience by encouraging them to confront and process difficult feelings and situations. Researchers at the University of California found that individuals who regularly engage in supportive conversations show decreased activation in the dorsal anterior cingulate cortex and Brodmann's area 8—regions of the brain linked to distress and social rejection. They also found that this decreased activity appears to lower cortisol levels, highlighting how supportive verbal interactions contribute to emotional resilience when facing challenges.[13] This is why people who go through significant challenges, such as bereavement, divorce, or abuse, are often encouraged to join a support group where they can speak openly about their challenge and hear others do the same about theirs. These groups often have slogans like, "You don't have to go it alone," because, in general, we gain emotional resilience when we have strong, authentic support, which is often delivered through supportive conversations that inherently hinge upon language.

Another way that the psychology literature elucidates the boost in emotional resilience that comes from deep, authentic verbal interactions is through something called "ego strength." We've all heard of people with outsize egos, but a healthy person at least has a strong, substantial ego. In laymen's terms, this refers to a person's rational sense of themselves as a capable person that can rely on themselves to "keep it together" and find solutions in times of challenge. In psychodynamic psychotherapy, it's not uncommon for the therapist to report "lending their ego strength" to a client who is struggling. When the client is expressing feelings of helplessness or loss, the therapist's response typically communicates in some manner that they are "coming alongside" the client in a way that bolsters the client's coping skills. As discussed earlier, other psychodynamic literature refers to the therapist providing emotional "containment" or a "secure base" for clients who are struggling.[14] These psychodynamic terms, along with the prevalence of colloquial phrases to describe feeling emotionally unburdened by meaningful verbal communication, like "getting something off your chest" or having a "heart to heart," underscore the point that emotional resilience is increased through deep, authentic verbal interaction.

Open dialogue boosts resilience by allowing us to:

- Face discomfort rather than suppress it
- Strengthen self-efficacy by fostering a sense of agency and containment around emotions
- Use emotions as a prosocial way and borrow from the ego-strength of our support system

5.   Reducing Anxiety and Depression

The role of language in reducing anxiety and depression through cognitive restructuring and other cognitive-based interventions is discussed in the Cognitive Gifts of Language chapter. But the role of language in reducing anxiety and depression is included here in the Emotional Gifts of Language chapter because, of course, there is an emotional aspect to anxiety and depression. Separating cognition and emotion is, in some sense, a false dichotomy since they are so deeply entwined: cognitive behavioral therapists certainly deal with emotion, and psychodynamic or psychoanalytic psychologists absolutely address the issue of cognition. But in general, both psychodynamic and psychoanalytic psychologists would posit that in many cases, our cognitions may be shaped by our unconscious emotional life, not the other way around. This is why the Cognitive Gifts of Language section of "Reducing Anxiety and Depression" focused on Cognitive behavioral approaches to therapy, and here in the Emotional Gifts of Language we'll focus more on psychodynamic therapy's approach to language for treatment of anxiety and depression. However, both schools of thought encompass both cognition and emotion.

While cognitive behavioral therapy focuses primarily upon how our cognitive processes shape our emotions, psychodynamic therapists often use language to do a deeper dive into the emotions themselves, including emotions within the unconscious or, in psychoanalytic terms, the id. For example, a psychodynamic therapist might be interested in a person's schema just like a cognitive behavioral therapist, but they would likely be interested in how those schemata were developed on a foundational level before the person developed verbal skills. Psychoanalytic psychologist John Bowlby developed the concept of the mother as a "secure base" whose consistent and emotionally attuned presence was essential for the healthy emotional development of infants and toddlers. Bowlby locates her as the foundation of the person's future "attachment style," which is integral to a person's schema or worldview.[15]

A person with an anxious attachment style would, naturally, be vulnerable to social anxiety disorder, so the attachment-oriented psychodynamic* psychologist might look at the same socially anxious patient described in the "Reducing Anxiety and Depression" section of the Cognitive Gifts of Language chapter and become curious about more than just the fact that the patient may have learned that the world was a judgmental place because the mother was critical. An attachment-oriented therapist might look deeper into the patient's early relationship with her mother: Was her mother reliably there for her, and attuned to her needs during infancy and early childhood? Was she left in her crib to cry for hours, or did her mother arrive promptly to comfort her? On the other hand, did her mother hover intrusively, thereby guiding the girl to sense that she couldn't function without the incessant support of her mother? How did all this shape the patient's orientation to the world, and how does that orientation affect her now?

---

*   Psychoanalytic psychology is often thought of as the father of the more modern psychodynamic psychology. The finer points of the distinctions between the two isn't particularly important here—for the purposes of this section, just understand that psychodynamic and psychoanalytic psychology are closely related, and both typically include an emphasis on unconscious emotion that is not typically part of cognitive behavioral therapy.

Because much of the history queried above occurred before the client was verbal (or able to use words in a skilled and precise manner), the work of psychodynamic therapy often involves getting in touch with the unconscious and putting it into language so that the client's deep inner world can be contained, examined, and understood. Psychodynamic therapy goals and processes are often less linear and more difficult to describe succinctly than cognitive behavioral therapy's goals and processes, partly because psychodynamic therapy often addresses the unconscious and strives to unpack the meaning derived from early childhood experiences—nevertheless, the process hinges on language. Psychodynamic therapy uses language for goals and techniques include, but are not limited to:

- **A corrective emotional experience**: To build on the example of the socially anxious patient whose mother was unreliable and thereby contributed to the patient developing a general sense of skittishness around feeling socially supported, a psychodynamic therapist might spend countless hours helping the client to get in touch with the socially anxious component of her worldview and examine how it became crystallized. This is partly why there is a cliché of therapists constantly saying "Tell me about your mother"—there is, generally, an assumption by psychodynamic therapists that the client has long-buried memories of wounding experiences, perhaps even preverbal, that are shaping the client's current experience and causing distress. By getting in touch with these memories and then responding to the client's distress differently than the mother did, a "corrective emotional experience" is attained and symptoms are reduced. For example, the socially anxious client might suddenly remember, after many hours in therapy, a time when her mother was hours late to pick

her up from preschool and then belittled her (then a little girl) for crying and being scared. The therapist would
respond compassionately to this memory and normalize
the need for the mother to have responded in a more
reassuring way. This process uses language to coax unconscious memories into light, provide emotional containment, and help reshape the client's sense of the world as a
scary place where people can't be trusted, thereby reducing
her social anxiety.

- **The provision of a "secure base"**: While the ideal situation, according to Bowlby and many who followed him,
was for the mother to be the "secure base" whom the
child could count on to be physically present and emotionally attuned (but not hovering—the mother had to
strike a balance between being consistently present without being intrusive) the therapist can help to fill this role
retroactively if the client experienced what Bowlby called
"maternal deprivation" or other disruptions to the ideal
secure base. This can be accomplished partly through the
therapist simply being there at the appointed time and
date (of course this requires language to establish), and
through the therapist demonstrating emotional attunement to the client over a large body of therapy sessions—
the demonstration of attunement hinges largely on the
therapist's *verbal* responses that indicate she has grasped
and understood the client's emotional experiences and is
able to contain them without being intrusive or aloof.

- **Reauthoring, Deconstructing, Externalizing, and
Narrative Building**: These techniques are grouped together
for the sake of space, as they are all part of Narrative
Therapy. The word "narrative" derives from Latin "narrati-
vus," which means "to tell a story." As the name implies,
the work of Narrative Therapy consists of helping the

client to examine their conscious or unconscious "story of their life," deconstruct it; reconsider the meanings they've attached to certain components of their life story; deliberately redefine many problems or challenges as external to the client rather than part of the client (this often involves giving the problems names or labels to underscore them as separate entities from the client); and then "reauthor" the story by creating a revised narrative that feels more empowering to the client. As you can see, the storytelling process of Narrative Therapy hinges almost entirely on the use of language.

Conclusion on the Cognitive and Emotional Gifts of Language

Language brings a nearly endless array of cognitive and emotional gifts. Although they are discussed here in separate categories for cognition and emotion, these gifts obviously complement one another and even overlap in many aspects. Cognition and emotion are typically separate units in psychology courses, but in many ways it's a false dichotomy—psychologists don't fully understand where one ends and the other begins. What we do know is that gaining control over our words and using that power to facilitate expression helps us think clearly, binds us together socially, helps us to self-regulate, and in fact can be healing—even when we're using language privately, with just a pen and paper. For example, researchers found that participants who had suffered a traumatic event had significantly higher scores on measures of post-traumatic growth and a greater ability to find adaptive meaning in their experience when they were guided to do an expressive writing exercise, compared to doing a neutral writing exercise.[16] There is a nearly bottomless well of literature in both psychodynamic and cognitive behavioral psychology demonstrating the healing power of words, but of course language has myriad benefits in our everyday lives far outside of a clinician's therapy office.[17, 18]

The gift of language is so profound and interwoven into almost every aspect of our lives that it becomes, ironically, easy to overlook. It is like the air we breathe, in that it is essential to our existence yet it is strikingly easy to take for granted unless something disrupts our access to use it freely.

Chapter 3

The Hidden Dangers of Self-Censorship

Much unhappiness has come into the world because of bewilderment and things left unsaid.
—FYODOR DOSTOEVSKY

The cognitive and emotional gifts of language are spectacular, but what happens when that natural and miraculous process of expression is interrupted? When we suppress the gifts of language, the psychological consequences can be profound. When we habitually censor ourselves on matters that are important to us, it becomes more than just a trivial social accommodation designed to deftly avoid unnecessary conflict. Habitual self-censorship on matters that are important to us is the stifling of an essential, uniquely human process that appears to be essential to our intellectual, emotional, and social well-being.

Before we go further, let's briefly unpack the terms "matters that are important to us" and "self-censorship."

Matters That Are Important to Us

What are the "matters that are important to us" that are often candidates for self-censorship because their discussion can lead to conflict? This is different for every person, of course, but political issues naturally tend to rank high on the list, even if a person doesn't think of themselves as "being into politics." This is because "politics" merely means our personal positions about the standards in our community.[1] In my experience as a psychologist, these topics often include things like abortion, welfare spending, climate change, education, DEI, religion, firearms, safety and crime, gender and sexuality, race relations, or border issues. To clarify, I'm not suggesting that *all* these topics are important to all people, but in my experience and in large-scale polls, at least one or two of these topics are typically important to most people. Even people who say they "don't do politics" tend to become riled if laws are passed that limit their freedoms, spike their taxes, or regulate behaviors in ways they dislike (such as limiting their gun ownership or irresponsibly empowering their "crazy neighbors" with questionable backgrounds to purchase a closetful of AR-15s). The old saying, "You may not do politics, but politics will do you," captures the fact that politics are inherently inescapable for anyone living in the civilized world. Even people who choose to live in remote areas where they are largely disconnected from daily interaction with a broad community depend upon political structures that protect their freedom to live in peaceful, undisturbed privacy. Politics intrinsically connects to societal controls, so it is one issue that uniquely affects us all—we all live in a society where we are subject to *some* sort of external governance or "politics," even if we don't necessarily think of it that way.

Self-Censorship

What does it mean to "self-censor" about politics? Don't people sometimes just keep things private? Isn't that part of having good boundaries? Yes, people often keep their personal life some-what private in workplace situations, and they avoid droning on about work at the neighborhood barbecue, or about private family dynamics during Monday morning meetings. It's normal to exer-cise a bit of self-restraint and situational awareness around these topics. But politics or politically adjacent topics are unique in that they are often off-limits in both the workplace and many personal relationships where private and sensitive information is other-wise shared somewhat freely. These topics are often candidates for self-censorship because people fear being canceled or ostracized if they express disagreement with whatever they perceive to be the "politically correct" viewpoint. Many therapists, me included, note that it's typically easier for clients to share about traditionally taboo topics like sex and money than about politics if they fear you may disagree with their political views. Other clients make flip political comments that convey an assumption their therapist agrees with them, which often leads to uniquely difficult pondering by the therapist on if and how to clarify the client's assumption—more so than if, for example, the client said something that conveyed an assumption that the therapist was athletic. This is because politics connects to values and to laws that ultimately govern our behavior, so discussion related to politically tinged topics can feel loaded, especially if the client seems prone to "canceling."

As we explore how self-censoring around these topics can have unintended consequences, let's briefly define the term "self-censorship": The difference between self-censorship and self-restraint is unpacked further in part 2, but for now suffice it to say that self-censorship is when you are hiding your views on a rigid, ongoing basis, sometimes even from people to whom you're rather close. Self-restraint is just the healthy, occasional choice to be judicious and sensitive about when and where you share per-sonal information, such as refraining from telling everyone at the board meeting about last night's marital argument.

Now that we know what self-censorship is and why politics is a domain that sometimes evokes it, let's understand why it can be dangerous to stifle ourselves around topics that matter to us. Many of us may avoid expressing our political views just to "be polite," or we may even actively hide our views without realizing that there are potential harms to this approach, if taken too far. (For example, by laughing at jokes about political figures or caricatures of political issues that we don't think are funny, to avoid being "outed.") While previous chapters explored the cognitive and emotional gifts of language, this chapter explores the problematic psychological processes that can arise when we interrupt the normal, healthy process of using language to organize and regulate our interior life and to build bridges between ourselves and others—especially if we are stifling this process around expressing viewpoints about the basic social standards and legal rules that shape our everyday lives.

Here are five hidden dangers of self-censorship:

1.   Overreliance on Maladaptive Defenses
Suppression, Repression, and Denial
When we stifle our speech, laugh at political barbs we don't actually think are funny to avoid making waves, or otherwise deny the truth of how we feel, we're likely engaging in what psychologists call suppression. Suppression is the conscious attempt to "push down" thoughts. For example, let's say Kayla, a student at a university class in gender studies, might initially feel inclined during a lecture on how "women are oppressed by the patriarchy" to explain to her professor that she actually feels quite empowered, and that she really enjoys being around men who are strong and protective in a traditionally masculine way, but she consciously decides *not* to do this out of a concern that it might negatively affect her rapport with the professor and ultimately hurt her grade.[2] When the professor makes casual asides

that are intended to be humorous, like, "Men are pigs," or "If you want to get something done, ask a woman," that Kayla finds insulting to her brothers and father, she bites her tongue and tries to look agreeable. She's just doing what psychologists call "impression management," as she knows a large part of her grade will be down to the professor's subjective regard for her essays and class participation. If she does this frequently and habitually, the suppression may develop into repression, which is when the suppression process becomes so automatic that the thoughts are eventually pushed into the unconscious and we no longer need to suppress them because they are "pre-suppressed" and don't even rise to consciousness as often or easily as before. At that point, Kayla might just sit in class letting her mind wander to other topics or simply focus on noting down the professor's key points so she can regurgitate them on the exam, but she's no longer thinking about the material in an engaged, critical manner.

At the repression stage, Kayla can likely still reconnect with her true views if someone were to elicit them in a manner that made her feel safe. For example, if another student confided during a study hall that she felt alienated by the professor's rather callous form of feminism, Kayla's eyes might brighten as she affirms feeling the same. However, if the classroom pattern continues long enough without interruption or opportunity to reconnect with her true views, it may begin to pervade other areas of Kayla's life. For example, she accepts invitations to apply for internship programs designed specifically to recruit women, and she's required to describe ways that she has "overcome sexism" during her interviews. The longer and more frequently that Kayla performs her way through these classes and internship programs that seem to require her to display a certain ideological perspective to be successful, Kayla might start to experience what psychologists call "denial." At this point, she has been pretending—or "going along to get along"—for so long that she's begun to dissociate from the parts of herself deemed "unacceptable" within repressively femi-nist environments. She earns top grades in gender studies, serves on the Women's Issues Committee at her internship, and lives with a self-identified "radical feminist" roommate. Immersed in this world, she's likely experiencing cognitive dissonance (a psy-chological maneuver where we unconsciously adjust our beliefs, at least on a surface level, in order to fit our behaviors). To resolve this tension, Kayla may reason that she must genuinely believe in the feminist rhetoric because she is so deeply embedded in the feminist network.

At this stage, a single comment in study hall wouldn't be enough for Kayla to reconnect with the buried part of herself; she might simply shrug and return to her studies or even dismiss the other student as naive. The repeated suppression, then repression, of her original views can eventually harden into a disconnected state of denial where Kayla has a hard time "remembering" the self she worked to hide. This process of decreasing self-awareness is also described in terms of the transition from normative social pressure to full-on cognitive dissonance, as outlined in item 5 of this chapter, Intellectual Deprivation.

Passive Aggression and Acting Out

When we're in denial, we're not in touch with our real views. This makes it hard to meet our needs and makes us vulnerable to pas-sive aggression. For example, Kayla might enter into a romantic relationship with a man who identifies as a feminist and goes to great pains to treat Kayla accordingly—he makes sure never to open the door for her, he splits the check when they're on dates, and he always asks for consent before initiating sex. He rarely goes to the gym except for yoga and makes fun of "jocks" who pound their chests and "act like animals" by the free weights. Because she is so deep into her denial, Kayla joins her boyfriend when he openly spurns traditional men as "toxically masculine," yet she also finds herself always feeling vaguely bored and irritated by her boy-friend. She's snippy and condescending toward him and secretly rolls her eyes at him for tolerating it. Yet whenever he becomes assertive or suggests she shouldn't go to a late-night party by her-self because he's concerned for her safety, she swats him down and chides him for "mansplaining," "controlling me," or "acting like such a stereotypical man." This dynamic is rife with passive aggression: Kayla doesn't like what her boyfriend is doing, but she can't communicate it directly, so her displeasure is communicated in backhanded and irrational ways. It sounds ridiculous, but it's quite normal: When we are prevented from dealing with problems in a direct manner, we resort to passive aggression.

We sometimes resort to passive aggression when we're mak-ing a conscious effort to avoid direct aggression (for example, smiling and nodding when dealing with an irritable and incom-petent repairman, while privately planning to call his supervisor to complain and request a refund later). But we can also fall prey to passive aggression when we've become unconscious of certain elements of ourselves, like Kayla's disconnection from the part of herself that was seeking a strong, traditional, protective man. She can't deal with the situation directly by telling her boyfriend how she really feels about his feminist-oriented treatment of her because she won't let *herself* face the truth, so her displeasure is expressed in an irrational, passive-aggressive manner. When we're conscious of our passive aggression (such as the repairman exam-ple), it can be adaptive, since there are situations in life where direct aggression is not advisable and the indirect or "passive" approach works best. But when passive aggression derives from a lack of awareness, it's usually less rational and less adaptive.

Eventually, Kayla's passive aggression may grow into what psy-chologists call "acting out." This is when Kayla's relatively minor irrational verbal swipes graduate into more dramatic behaviors, often marked by a greater disconnection from reality, such as through fantasy or exaggerated versions of what we'd seek if we were consciously in touch with our desires. For example, Kayla begins a flirtatious pattern of interaction with the night-shift study hall janitor, Paul, an ex-convict who is quite different from Kayla's boyfriend. He's working on turning his life around, but he's still extremely rough around the edges and his outsized muscular build makes it clear that he still adheres to the same ironman weightlifting routine that kept him at the top of the food chain in a perilous prison social environment. Kayla won't admit it to herself, but she finds him quite attractive. She wouldn't label her interaction with him as flirtatious, but an outside observer would see all the signs (she flips her hair, giggles, and even starts paying a little extra attention to the way she dresses when heading to the evening study hall). Her boyfriend commented on this once, but Kayla read him the riot act and told him to keep his "cis white male privilege in check and stop trying to police my behavior."

Truth be told, Paul is a little "over the top," even if Kayla were fully in touch with herself. His masculine tendency for risk-taking obviously went a bit haywire and landed him in prison, and his masculine willingness to fight went beyond being adaptive and protective (he confided in Kayla that he had served time for aggravated assault with a deadly weapon as part of organized gang activity). But because Kayla isn't in touch with what she's missing from her boyfriend, or that she's "acting out" her unconscious desire by flirting with Paul, she can't evaluate the situation rationally. If she could, she'd probably break up with her boyfriend, find a more traditional-yet-safe man, and never have struck up this "blind flirtation" with Paul in the first place.

Paul finally works up his nerve and asks Kayla if she'd like to go out sometime. This nearly forces Kayla to confront the reality that she's been "acting out" a dynamic where she basks in the attention of this caricatured-masculine man. However, because she's operating from a place of denial, she can't see the situation clearly, and she certainly can't acknowledge that she participated in a flirtation that led to Paul asking her out. So, Kayla recoils and labels Paul as "creepy." She operates in an unconscious fantasy world where she was innocently going to study hall, and Paul harassed her with unwanted sexual advances that objectified her. In this way, Kayla has "acted out" her desire for a man who is the extreme opposite of the boyfriend she has selected, because she won't permit herself to acknowledge what she *really* wants and pursue a more balanced relationship. In other words, Kayla isn't being purposely manipulative or dishonest; she's just so disconnected from certain parts of herself that her actions have become distorted through suppression, repression, denial, passive aggression, and acting out.

Kayla's experience might seem extreme, and of course it's dramatized to illustrate psychological processes in clear, bright lines, but it's not as far-fetched as it might sound. We all have psychological processes like Kayla's that operate outside of our awareness, even on the most basic level. For example, have you ever only realized how hungry you were when you paused for a moment in the middle of a big project and suddenly your brain realized that you're ravenous? It isn't that your body suddenly became hungry; it's that your brain blocked awareness of it to focus on other things. Have you ever watched a friend insist that "everything is fine," obviously lying even to themselves, when they're clearly upset? We're all capable of pulling the wool over our own eyes and, as discussed earlier in the context of repression and passive aggression, these defenses can sometimes be adaptive. The key is to remain vigilant so that this process doesn't distort our perception of reality to the point of becoming counterproductive. The slippery slope toward acting out and denial often begins with the self-censorship of our true thoughts. Self-censorship, often beginning as a subtle form of repression, can quickly evolve into suppression, eventually paving the way for unhealthy levels of passive aggression, denial, and emotional acting out. What may begin as a harmless "white lie" to preserve rapport can escalate rapidly. A little social finesse is perfectly normal, and even useful—but it's crucial to recognize the risk of allowing a benign social script to morph into full-blown cognitive dissonance.

2. Increased Vulnerability to Violence

Not only are we setting the stage to respond to words with physical violence when we take the phrase "words are violence" literally, but we may also increase our likelihood of "acting out" through violence by suppressing speech, since words are often an excellent alternative to violence. When working with hardened criminals who have a dangerous propensity toward violence or even a young child who bonks his brother for taking his toy, common sense and psychological literature guide us to teach the perpetrator to "use your words."[3, 4, 5, 6, 7] As we know from the Cognitive and Emotional Gifts of Language chapters, verbal expression helps to decrease amygdala activity, enhance problem-solving skills, and create detachment between ourselves and our ideas, thereby making it easier to analyze and discard maladaptive ideas. These features alone make it nonsensical to limit people's ability to use words to navigate or define their positions about societal flashpoints. Ironically, the more we censor "problematic" speech, the more we might foster violence by forcing people into the shadows with material that needs to be expressed and explored. Strict speech codes don't really *stop* speech, they just force people to express or explore forbidden ideas in a clandestine manner, likely with fewer checks or challenges, and may make them more vulnerable to acting out with violence.

Subverting free speech in an attempt to create a more peaceful society could actually increase vulnerability to violence by weakening individuals' ability to resolve conflicts verbally and reinforcing impulsive, aggressive responses. Research on impulsive aggression indicates that language processing and verbal reasoning play a critical role in modulating aggression, as those with stronger language skills are better equipped to engage in self-regulation, cognitive restraint, and conflict resolution without resorting to violence. Suppressing speech—especially dissenting or controversial ideas—can lead to frustration, misinterpretation of intent, and a diminished ability to verbally negotiate disagreements, potentially increasing defensive rage responses and escalating physical aggression. Rather than creating a more harmonious society, restricting open dialogue may deprive people of the linguistic and cognitive tools necessary to de-escalate conflicts, making them more susceptible to reactive violence when confronted with opposing views. As Daryl Davis, the black R&B singer who has convinced dozens of KKK members to surrender their hoods (discussed in chapter 4), said in an interview with Al Jazeera, "When two enemies are talking, they are not fighting, they are talking. It's when the conversation ceases that the ground becomes fertile for violence. So, you want to keep the conversation going."[8]

3. Degraded Social Support
Weakened Social Connections
When we stifle ourselves and mask our true feelings, relationships feel tenuous and the quality of our social support is, naturally, degraded. We can't get support with what we're experiencing if we hide our feelings. Moreover, hiding our feelings requires effort, and it creates an ongoing cloud of apprehension that our "real feelings" might slip and become known. It's natural to curate how we present ourselves to others to a certain degree. Psychologists call this "impression management," and it is actually adaptive insofar as it helps us to observe basic social norms and relate in a manner that is considerate to others. However, if taken too far, we can feel as if we're presenting a "false self." When

we mask our true feelings, we make it harder to get meaningful support from others—and they find it harder to get meaningful support from us.[9]

Open dialogue can create (or is created by) spaces where individuals feel able to share their true selves and have emotional connections that are authentic, deep, and vulnerable. Our cortisol levels (described colloquially as "the stress hormone") naturally drop when we're with trusted friends and family.[10] This is why truly "safe spaces" are those where we can "keep it real," trusting that we are known and loved for who we are, and that our bonds are strong enough to withstand disagreement. In fact, communication is so deeply entwined with our sense of community that these words actually share the same Latin root, *communis*, or "shared."

Shutting People Out and the Epidemic of Loneliness

When people censor themselves, conversations become shallow, leading to surface-level relationships that lack authenticity. As discussed in the Introduction, we are in an epidemic of loneliness. Many patients have told me they are surrounded by people, yet they feel lonely because so few people really know them; their interactions are superficial at best and contrived or deliberately (defensively) inauthentic at worst. While their complaint of low relationship quality is valid, they often have to acknowledge that the isolation of their "real self" is self-imposed. They are choosing to hide much of their real views because they fear the rejection that could arise if their views create separation between themselves and others. Ironically, they actually create the separation they fear. By preemptively depriving others of the chance to know the "real" them, they shut down opportunities to find middle ground, discover that others agree with them, or find that they can "agree to disagree."

Psycholinguist Steven Pinker has said that language connects us "like a network" where we can plug into our community. Indeed, we do call it "networking" when we support each other in one of the most basic human needs, the need to work (Pinker 2007).[11] Psychologists also refer to a "support network" when evaluating the ever-crucial social network available to a person under stress. In many ways, plugging into that network is key to our survival. My concern is that suppressing ourselves mentally or otherwise stifling our gift of language is like trying to connect to a network with a frayed wire—we might be able to make a connection, but the connection is unreliable, bumpy, tenuous, and frustrating. Again, it's normal to curate what we share with others to a certain degree—we don't need to share *everything with everyone, all the time.* But when we feel we have to hide our thoughts on topics that matter (and, as discussed earlier, politics is just another word for "values about the community"), we are hiding a fundamental part of ourselves—especially if the habit of self-censorship bleeds into our circles of family and friends.

The Illusion of "Safe Spaces"

Misguided efforts to create "safe spaces" often thwart efforts at genuine dialogue. True safety lies in allowing diverse opinions to be shared without fear of retribution.

True "safe spaces" are places where diverse opinions can be shared openly, without fear of retribution or suppression. Even the term "safe space" implies that other spaces without certain ideological speech controls are "unsafe." Haidt expires how this can lead to fragility in *The Coddling of the American Mind.*[12] and he's right. But I have also seen it lead to more of the "fight" side of the fight-or-flight response that arises when we feel unsafe. The safety-ism of micromanaged safe spaces likely fosters neuroticism at best and a maladaptive tendency toward violence to "defend" from the "unsafe" elements at worst.

Erosion of Self-Efficacy and Self-Esteem → Increased Vulnerability to Depression and Anxiety

Speech is frequently a precursor of actions. Just as speech helps us organize our thoughts, it can also help us to verbally commit to a course of action.[13] The ability to "do what we say we're going to do" is what psychologists call "self-efficacy." It reflects our belief in our ability to find and utilize coping skills for survival and to meet our needs. As you can imagine, self-efficacy is tied to self-esteem, but it's slightly different. It's more action oriented. In fact, increasing self-efficacy has been shown to raise self-esteem. This makes sense; of course it's a boost to know you can count on yourself.[14, 15] Not surprisingly, low self-efficacy has been strongly tied to diagnoses of depression and anxiety. Just like the healthy function of anxiety is to stimulate productive preparation behaviors, the hallmark symptom of depression is a sense of helplessness or hopelessness, so naturally self-efficacy plays a key role.

The connection between self-efficacy, anxiety, and depression is striking. If for some reason we are unable to think clearly and tap our support network to help us determine and carry out constructive preparation behaviors, of course we feel helpless and become depressed. In an almost circular sense, lethargy is a symptom of depression (and lethargy would, of course, disrupt your ability to do preparation behaviors, placing depressed individuals at risk of spiraling deeper into depression). Similarly, irritability and isolation are symptoms of depression. The preceding section on the erosion of social support becomes part of the "mental health spiral" as well. Speech is not just a means of communication; it is an essential tool for developing self-efficacy. By verbalizing our thoughts, committing to actions, and engaging in supportive conversations, we strengthen our ability to navigate challenges. When we're speaking openly with others, we enjoy a positive circular interaction with our self-efficacy and mental well-being—and decrease our vulnerability to anxiety or depression.

When individuals consistently suppress their thoughts, they may experience anxiety or depression because they can't face problems and deal with them directly. This, in turn, can create a negative feedback loop, where increasing anxiety and depression further impair their ability to manage stressors. As a result, their self-efficacy (belief in their ability to handle challenges) may decline. A negative spiral is then created as decreased self-efficacy makes it harder to overcome anxiety and depression, which can pose challenges to self-efficacy. Research supports this, showing that self-efficacy plays both a mediating and a moderating role in the relationship between depression and anxiety.[16, 17]

As discussed in the Cognitive Gifts of Language chapter, the mere act of speaking can frequently be productive in terms of mental clarity and cognitive functioning. Interestingly, feeling mentally sluggish or struggling with racing thoughts are symptoms of depression and anxiety respectively. Kayla illustrates the connection as well between suppression's disrupting effect upon speech and hurting our ability to face reality and solve problems. Countless patients have discussed how good it felt just to "talk things through," or how much they valued the accountability they knew our sessions provided. Once they'd said they were going to try a technique, they felt committed and more likely to follow through. In other words, their self-efficacy seemed to increase, and increasing self-efficacy has been demonstrated to help individuals suffering from depression or anxiety.[18]

Finally, when we habitually suppress our thoughts and feelings in deference to others, we're behaviorally signaling to ourselves that our internal experience doesn't really matter. We're putting our own needs aside to make space for others without a sense of reciprocity. This is associated with low self-esteem and codependency, both of which are associated with depression. Psychological techniques like Behavioral Activation include speaking up even if it doesn't feel comfortable, with the idea that we can activate a healthier mental state through performing the *behaviors* of a healthier person. In a reverse sense, by taking on the behaviors of a person with low self-esteem (such as stifling our thoughts because we don't feel they are worthy of expression, or because the feelings of others matter more than our own), we may cultivate the low self-esteem that is clearly associated with depression and anxiety.

The relationships between anxiety, depression, self-efficacy, and self-esteem are circular and interconnected, but the basic idea is that talking things through (or at least writing things down in private) can help us to advocate for ourselves through verbally committing to constructive actions. Putting your thoughts and feelings into words (even just by journaling) can boost your ability to take constructive action and reduce vulnerability to anxiety or depression.

Moreover, the eroded social support described in the preceding section would constitute an additional risk factor for anxiety and depression. As you can see, the factors of compromised mental clarity due to repression and denial, decreased self-efficacy and self-esteem, and degraded social support could combine and exacerbate one another—and they all connect back to stifling speech.

Intellectual Deprivation

The Cognitive Gifts of Language chapter unpacked the myriad intellectual benefits of language. When we interrupt speech, do we simply lose access to those gifts? In fact, something worse happens. Just like interrupting speech does more than simply deprive us of the emotional benefits of language (it creates a liability by distorting them into suppression, repression, denial, and other *problems* outlined in previous sections of this chapter), interrupting our normal process of using speech to express ourselves clearly and accurately is associated with counterproductive cognitive processes. In other words, depriving ourselves of speech isn't like hitting the "pause button" on benefits, because it's more likely to take a toll on our mind. We can create disturbances in the accurate exchange of information, make ourselves vulnerable to cognitive distortions, and ultimately even facilitate groupthink. Here are some examples of psychology studies and concepts that build on each other to show how this process works, culminating in real-life groupthink results that illustrate the incredible extent to which we can fool ourselves en masse.

A. "Normative Social Pressure": In a classic 1951 study known as the Asch Line Experiment, psychologist Solomon Asch led a team of researchers who simply showed a roomful of participants three lines and asked them to select which line was closest in length to a comparison line.* However, it wasn't actually a roomful of participants—it was a roomful of researchers posing as participants, and one actual participant. The actual participant was always placed second to last in the response sequence, so that he would observe dozens of "participants" before him indicating the same incorrect response. Researchers found that about 75 percent of participants would "go with the crowd" and indicate the same incorrect response. Psychologists call this "normative social pressure."

You might wonder if the participants *actually* "psyched themselves out" and believed the incorrect response, or if they were aware of the correct response but just giving in to social pressure. When asked directly about the situation post-test, participants said they knew the truth and were just giving in to social pressure. However, this experiment

---

* The researchers deliberately made the answer so obvious that less than 1 percent of people were confirmed to have any difficulty responding accurately under normal circumstances, so that they could accurately isolate the reason for performance difficulties.

illustrates how easily the authenticity of our factual communication can be degraded when we feel pressured into social conformity. It's also possible that when we say things that are untrue, we will come to believe what we're saying even if we initially knew we were being untruthful. In other words, we can "drink our own Kool-Aid" and distort our thought process by verbally pretending our thought process is different than what it is. In the Asch line experiment, participants were essentially guided to retrace their cognitive steps, and *then* they spoke clearly about their thought process. But what if this cognitive debriefing process hadn't been made so easy for them? What if there had been a touch of subjectivity involved, with more room to fool themselves? Psychologists addressed *this* possibility in the years following the Asch line experiment and discovered something called cognitive dissonance.

B. Cognitive Dissonance: In 1959, psychologist Leon Festinger built on the work of Asch. He ran an experiment to see if we sometimes change our thought process to accommodate our speech and behavior (in psychology, speech is considered a behavior). He had research participants come in one at a time and do a long, boring task (the task had actually been selected through other experiments designed to create a task that would almost universally be rated as boring). Once they completed the boring task, and believed the "experiment" was over, Festinger asked them to tell the next participant in line that the experiment was fun and interesting. Festinger had two experimental conditions: In the first, he offered the participant $1 to "talk up" the experiment. In the second condition, he offered the participant $20 to do it (in 1959, $20 was a considerable sum). After the participant had "talked up" the experiment to the next person and received their money, Festinger asked them what they really thought of the task. Participants who were paid $1 rated the task as more enjoyable than participants who had been paid more; participants who were paid $20 remained conscious of the fact that the experiment was actually boring, and acknowledged that they had lied in order to get the money.

This is the seminal study that gave rise to the term "cognitive dissonance," which refers to the fact that we'll sometimes change our thoughts in order to close the dissonance between our thoughts and our speech behaviors. This means that if we say things that we don't believe just because it's easier to parrot politically correct talking points than to speak up for what we really believe, we may fool ourselves and ultimately distort our own thought process around these topics.

C. Groupthink: Normative social pressure and cognitive dissonance set the table for groupthink to occur, especially if other conditions such as self-censorship are present. Groupthink is when a group becomes such an "echo chamber" that it becomes shockingly blind to incredibly obvious errors in its decision-making process, to the point where the group may ignore clear warnings from outside sources and blunder into deeply flawed decisions that appear self-evidently and blatantly wrong in retrospect.

The term "groupthink" was coined by psychologist Irvin Janis in 1972 as part of a report commissioned by the United States government to investigate how the Bay of Pigs disaster could possibly have been allowed to occur, given that a highly competent group of dedicated professionals had been working diligently on a special committee to plan the invasion. Groupthink has also been widely cited as an underlying reason behind the disastrously flawed decisions that led to the tragic explosion of the *Challenger* space shuttle. In both cases, by creating an environment where dissent was discouraged, intelligent individuals were led to suppress doubts and go along with flawed decisions. The illusion of unanimity and pressure to conform led to disastrous outcomes that likely could have been avoided if open dialogue and critical thinking had been encouraged. Both the *Challenger* and the Bay of Pigs are commonly cited in basic psychology textbooks as primary examples of groupthink (e.g., Griggs 2008[19]). As you can see, being intelligent or passionate about your goal or working toward a worthy cause are not protections against groupthink. Nobody is questioning the intelligence, goals, or dedication of the professionals responsible for these disasters. The culprit is groupthink.

"All silencing of discussion is an assumption of infallibility."
—John Stuart Mill, 1859

Janis listed eight conditions or symptoms of groupthink, and one of them is self-censorship. Another is the illusion of unanimity, which is naturally created when people start self-censoring any dissenting opinions. A third factor listed by Janis is "self-appointed mindguards," which would include many members of the "expert class" whose opinions or findings can seem untouchable. Whether it's the lofty college professor, a friend with a domineering personality who touts the latest study as if it's intellectual gospel to guide your life, an authoritative news anchor proclaiming that "the science is settled," or an overbearing boss who believes strongly in a particular new program, the presence of a "self-appointed mindguard" who seems beyond reproach can make speaking up very intimidating. Sometimes this strong normative social pressure can give way to cognitive dissonance where we start tinkering with our thought process in order to rationalize why we're going along with material that may seem quite questionable. At scale, this can culminate in groupthink.

Other factors that Janis listed include "direct pressure on dissenters," "outgroup stereotypes," and "belief in inherent morality of the group." It's easy to see how these factors map onto the well-intentioned individual who gets swept ever-deeper into heady rhetoric that results in cancel culture where old friends suddenly get the cold shoulder after making the "wrong" Facebook post, or parents receive a "going no contact letter" from their adult child after voting for the "wrong" candidate and being labeled as a "Nazi." At the extreme, it may result in somehow feeling justified in participating in episodes of violence such as the recent spate of attacks on Tesla dealerships and vehicles.*

Groupthink dynamics such as the illusion of unanimity are further amplified by a social media feed that is designed to serve the user with posts that echo his viewpoint. This was exacerbated when social media sites infamously "shadowbanned" conservative content but denied doing it, leading to a situation where millions of Americans simply thought their viewpoint must be an extreme outlier since it seemed so incredibly scarce on major social media platforms. Years later, Mark Zuckerberg of Meta and Elon Musk of X revealed that in many cases the government had pressured these platforms behind the scenes to de-amplify or altogether deplatform conservative content.[20, 21] To his credit, Zuckerberg apologized for his role in the secret censorship that occurred. Musk didn't apologize because he hadn't been connected to then

---

* A 2025 study from Rutgers University found that nearly 60 percent of respondents who identified as left of center indicated that destroying Tesla dealerships was at least partially acceptable.

Network Contagion Research Institute and Rutgers University Social Perception Lab, *Assassination Culture: How Burning Teslas and Killing Billionaires Became a Meme Aesthetic for Political Violence*, April 7, 2025, https://networkcontagion.us/wp-content/uploads/NCRI-Assassination -Culture-Brief.pdf.

Twitter (now X) when all of this occurred, but he did invite conservative content creators and independent-minded medical experts who had been affected by the shadowbanning into X headquarters to learn more about what had occurred, and he shared various emails as well as a private communication portal between (then) Twitter and the government in order to shine a light on what had previously occurred in the shadows.[22, 23, *]

---

*   Several studies have examined the visibility of conservative versus liberal content on X during the 2024 election. Some analyses indicate conservative content received a boost around the time its new owner Elon Musk endorsed Donald Trump. While some attribute this to algorithmic bias, others argue it merely reflects a correction of the previously acknowledged bias against conservative content under prior ownership. The platform had admitted to suppressing conservative content (sometimes at the request of government officials) under previous ownership; but has made no such admissions regarding liberal content under the current ownership. Studies from the University of Southern California, University of Queensland, and *The Washington Post* questioned whether conservative content has been unduly amplified under Musk's ownership. While they found no statistical evidence of liberal content being suppressed or "shadowbanned," their analyses did suggest that conservative content had received a boost compared to previous years. In contrast, *The Wall Street Journal* reported that political content from both sides was amplified equally.

    Stephanie Lee, "Researchers Uncover an Information Operation Threatening the 2024 U.S. Presidential Election," USC Viterbi School of Engineering, November 1, 2024, https://viterbischool.usc.edu/news/2024/11/information-operation-threatens-the-2024-u-s-presidential-election/.

    Timothy Graham and Mark Andrejevic, *A Computational Analysis of Potential Algorithmic Bias on Platform X During the 2024 US Election* (Brisbane: Queensland University of Technology, 2024), https://eprints.qut.edu.au/253211/.

    Drew Harwell and Jeremy B. Merrill, "On Elon Musk's X, Republicans Go Viral as Democrats Disappear," *The Washington Post*, October 29, 2024, https://www.washingtonpost.com/technology/2024/10/29/elon-musk-x-republican-democrat-twitter-election/.

    Jack Gillum, Alexa Corse, and Adrienne Tong, "X Algorithm Feeds Users Political Content—Whether They Want It or Not," *Wall Street Journal*, October 29, 2024, https://www.wsj.com/politics/elections/x-twitter-political-content-election-2024-28f2dadd.

The political skew of the examples provided for groupthink drives me to reiterate what I mentioned in the Introduction of this book: The examples are not intended to smear a particular side of the aisle, but in the current climate, people who identify as liberal are statistically much more likely to socially exclude conservatives than the reverse (see the "five Ds" described in the "Is this a Democrat versus Republican Issue?" section of the introduction), and major social media platforms *did* secretly suppress conservative voices during the 2020 election and the pandemic, as now openly acknowledged by Meta and X. As discussed throughout this book, silencing yourself or others can lead to loneliness and a host of other issues that affect mental health, and the long-standing mental health and happiness gaps between people on the right of the political spectrum has only widened since the rise of cancel culture, with liberals suffering the most. Being in denial of current problems and promoting irrational fears of free speech or conservative political viewpoints as "violence" may lead to lack of support for those who need it.[24, 25, 26, 27, 28]

Conclusion on The Dangers of Self-Censorship:

This chapter breaks the costs of subverting speech into categories like emotional, social, and cognitive; but of course, human experience isn't neatly partitioned into discrete categories; these areas overlap and affect each other. Just like the mind is a symphony of cognition, emotion, and social connection, all the factors described in this chapter can work in tandem to have exponential effects that can take a collective toll on our mental health and overall functioning. When individuals are silenced, whether by external forces or internal fear, they suffer, and society can suffer too.

When we censor ourselves (or require others to do so) out of a belief that certain viewpoints are so intolerable that "protection" from them is needed, we're signaling to ourselves and others that we (or they) are too fragile to endure disagreement or too feeble-minded to withstand exposure to ill-informed ideas. When we have the idea that mere exposure to certain words or ideas is tantamount to "violence" or creates a "threat to our existence," we are amping up our sense of vulnerability to the point of paranoia.

The good news is that, like the brave little boy who shouted, "The emperor has no clothes!" and broke the spell of groupthink that had his whole village worshipfully admiring the emperor's "clothes" (which were nonexistent), we can change the dynamics by speaking up and making space for others to do the same.

Chapter 4

Three Common Objections
to Free Speech

**Only through diversity of opinion is there . . . a chance
of fair play to all sides of the truth.**
—JOHN STUART MILL

Many intelligent, thoughtful people have offered carefully reasoned objections to free speech. For example, Katherine Maher, the CEO of National Public Radio (NPR), has said that the First Amendment is the "number one challenge" in combating disinformation online.[1] Former United States Secretary of State John Kerry said in 2024 that the First Amendment is "a major block" in "hammering [misinformation] out of existence."[2] A 2024 survey[3] found that more than a third of Americans believe that preventing hate speech is more important than protecting free speech (interestingly, Generation Y endorsed this belief most frequently at 42 percent, while Gen Z was significantly lower at 27 percent).

Whether we're talking about legal limits on speech, policy-based limits on speech at private companies or schools, or unspoken social codes about what is "unspeakable" in polite society, it's important to explore the valid criticisms of free speech in a variety of arenas.

As you read, you'll see that we already have clear legal guardrails in place; and many extralegal restrictions on free speech may actually have the opposite effect of what was intended. The goal is not to erase long-standing limits of free speech or encourage hateful speech. It's to have a basic understanding of our current legal framework and the potential unintended consequences of placing further limits beyond that framework, even with the best of intentions.

1.   What about hate speech and bullying? Isn't it better to create safe spaces?

Well-meaning people often suggest limiting speech to "combat hate" and "prevent bullying." While their intentions are admirable, they are often misguided. What they seem to overlook is that silencing people can be a form of hatred and bullying as well. Robbing people of their right to speak is fundamentally invalidating and disempowering. Moreover, when people are prohibited from expressing themselves plainly and directly, they are prone to resort to passive aggression. For example, male college students who are prohibited from openly discussing their frustration with the fact that women can sometimes fabricate false allegations of sexual misconduct (and that these false allegations can have devastating consequences for the accused) because such talk would be deemed as "hateful" or "misogynistic" might react to the suppression of their would-be protest by becoming generally insular and distrustful, and ultimately less inclusive of women. These men's passive-aggressive movement away from women, which is actually more divisive than their original impulse to have a civil discussion about a legitimate concern, occurs because they were prohibited from addressing the conflict openly and directly, so they resort to a passive-aggressive mode of responding.*

---

*   In 2016, at an annual meeting in Washington DC for the nonprofit Families Advocating for Campus Equality (FACE), I had the privilege of

(Continued)

Since prohibiting a person's right to speak their mind doesn't obliterate the thoughts they're having (it merely hides them) and often fosters passive-aggressive behaviors, we must also consider if it truly makes sense to believe that suppressing speech truly creates "safe spaces." For example, as a woman, I would much rather know if I were in a group that believed women were inferior. This knowledge would empower me to persuade them, distance myself, or respond in whatever way I chose. But an environment where nobody was allowed to verbalize their bias against women would not boost my empowerment; it would merely increase my sense of uncertainty. Truly safe spaces are those where differences can be discussed amicably.

Obviously, I'm not suggesting that I'd feel safe in a space where people advocated for violence against women. But our legal understanding of the First Amendment's conceptualization of free speech already prohibits incitement to violence (see Common Objection #2 on "SOME limits to speech" in chapter 4). I'm also not suggesting that I'd want to be surrounded by people who chattered incessantly about the inferiority of women. Free speech doesn't mean we have to lend our ears to anyone and everyone; it just means they have a right to say what they want. Moreover, allowing bad ideas (perhaps I'm biased, but I categorize the idea that women are inferior as a "bad idea") to be spoken actually helps to dispel them through open debate that exposes their flaws (see Common Objection #3 on misinformation).

Another reason why suppressing speech that is "hateful" or "bullying" can do more harm than good is that we can inadvertently undermine the self-esteem of the alleged victim by

---

meeting with a small group of about a dozen young men falsely accused of sexual misconduct who described this dynamic in painful detail. In many cases, they were suspended or expelled from school without even facing criminal charges or being able to face their accuser in a formal setting to defend themselves against the allegations.

colluding with the infantilizing idea that the victim is too fragile
to withstand words of opposition. In some cases, the suppression
even goes beyond "protecting" the alleged victim from ever having
to hear the words, and extends into the ability for the words to
be spoken at all. For example, Olivia Krolczyk, a college student
at the University of Cincinnati, received a failing grade for using
the term "biological woman" on a gender studies project proposal
about the potential harms of trans-identifying males participating
in women's sports. The professor, who was not trans-identifying,
issued a failing grade with a note that, "The terms 'biological
women' are exclusionary and are not allowed in this course as
they further reinforce heteronormativity." (Nelson 2023)[4]

As you can see, Ms. Krolczyk wasn't being prohibited from
using scientifically accurate language in the presence of anyone
who might *claim* to be victimized by it. Her scientifically accurate
language was deemed so dangerous that it couldn't even be used
in an academic proposal being read by a non-trans-identifying
professor for a project where the distinction between biological
women and trans-identifying males would be an integral part of
her proposed study (Prestigiacomo 2025).[*]

Prohibiting speech at this level colludes with a maladaptive
idea that the alleged victims of speech are *so* fragile that having
words of opposition used anywhere, even in contexts outside of
their earshot, is too threatening to be endured. This approach is

---

[*]   Notably, Ms. Krolczyk was subsequently prevented from speaking when
       violent Antifa protesters disrupted an attempted speaking engagement in
       2025 at the University of Washington. Her speech was ultimately shut
       down and she was escorted from the building by multiple police officers in
       full riot gear. She has since filed a civil rights complaint, which is still in
       process at the time of this writing.
            Amanda Prestigiacomo, "Exclusive: Conservative Rebuking Trans Ideology
       Was Silenced by Leftist Mob. Now She's Fighting Back," *The Daily Wire*,
       February 11, 2025, https://www.dailywire.com/news/exclusive-womens-rights
       -advocate-files-federal-complaint-after-being-silenced-on-campus.

the opposite of a resilience-promoting stance in which we assume that competent adults are strong enough to withstand verbal disagreement. It is no wonder that this approach has coincided with an increase in mental health problems. Obviously, there are many factors that underlie our mental health crisis, but as a psychologist, I am concerned that policies designed to validate the idea that "words are violence" create an unnecessary level of distress for the alleged victims and becomes a cudgel to silence speech that does not actually diminish the safety of others.

Such policies not only create an unnecessary level of distress for the alleged victims by instilling or reinforcing a belief that words are a "threat to their existence," they also create a perverse incentive for ideological opponents to construe themselves as victims of "hatred" or "bullying." If the consequence of speech being labeled as hateful is that the speaker is silenced, what better way to "win an argument" (or at least gain power over your opponent) than to shut down your opponent by labeling their speech as hateful? Who really holds more power in a dynamic where so-called "bullies" lose their right to speech? Psychologists use the term "secondary gains" to describe the benefits of a problem or illness. The classic textbook example is a child who becomes so attached to the cast on her broken leg because all her friends lovingly sign it for her, and she is excused from certain chores, that she insists the leg is not healed even when the doctor says it's time to remove the cast.

Sometimes, secondary gains are strong enough to incentivize an attachment to, or even fabrication of, a problem. I often wonder if a dynamic like this is at play when cries of "bullying" or "hate speech" are used to silence people or even used as a justification for violence. It's important to understand that falling into the trap of secondary gains can happen to anyone. It's not meant to be an accusation of a character flaw, and sometimes it's conscious, sometimes not. Here's an example from my clinical practice involving an employee in a high-pressure workplace who let go of a false bullying narrative and found deeper, more durable benefits than the short-term secondary gains that the old narrative had provided.

Vignette: Calista and the Secondary Gains of Victimhood

Early in my career, I worked as a counselor for a firm that provided employee assistance program (EAP) services. That's where I met Calista, a mid-level professional navigating a high-pressure corporate job. Her manager had initiated the referral out of concern for both her declining work performance and her ongoing complaints of being "bullied" by a colleague.

Calista arrived for her first session poised, articulate, and eager to frame the problem. "I'm not underperforming because I'm careless," she insisted. "I'm being bullied. That's why I'm so stressed all the time."

As she began describing the situation, the picture she painted didn't resemble traditional workplace bullying. Rather than repeated, targeted one-way aggression, the incidents Calista described were subtle, mutual, and often provoked. She claimed that a particular coworker made her feel self-conscious and excluded yet also shared that she had openly criticized that same coworker to others— mocking her work habits, suggesting she was "sterile" and "robotic," and sometimes initiating gossip about her.

The more I listened, the clearer it became that this was not a scenario of one employee victimizing another, but a case of relational conflict—a two-sided interpersonal dynamic marked by passive aggression, competitiveness, and escalating hostility. From an objective standpoint, Calista's own behavior clearly played a significant role in the tension, but she was heavily invested in portraying herself as the sole victim and kept referring to "the bully" to describe her colleague.

When I gently inquired about elements of her narrative that revealed the mutual quality of the antagonism between the two women, Calista admitted that she had been "harsh at times" but insisted her actions were defensive. "I'm only reacting to how I'm being treated in the first place," she said, with a shrug. "If she weren't so emotionally abusive, I wouldn't have to bite back."

There was no clear power imbalance, and no evidence of persistent or targeted harassment. Yet Calista remained fixed on the *bullying* label. This attachment to victimhood raised important clinical questions about secondary gains—the unconscious psychological benefits a person might receive from maintaining a symptom, narrative, or conflict.

In Calista's case, one of those gains seemed to be relief from workplace expectations. Her bullying claims had resulted in a pause on performance evaluations and shielded her from formal accountability while the situation was being "investigated." While there was no indication that she had fabricated her distress, there was clear resistance to solutions that could have improved her circumstances—such as setting boundaries with the coworker, disengaging from gossip, or enlisting HR support in neutral ways.

Why would someone resist straightforward interventions to reduce a conflict they claim is causing them harm?

One of the most clinically significant answers lies in the concept of secondary gains. As explained earlier, secondary gains are the unintended psychological or practical benefits a person receives from maintaining a symptom, behavior, or narrative—often without conscious awareness. In Calista's case, the role of "bullying victim" provided her with a powerful form of protection: it shifted attention away from her underperformance and insulated her from formal consequences. As long as the focus remained on interpersonal mistreatment, she was spared from confronting deeper anxieties about competence and capability. Secondary gains can be deceptively reinforcing. Even when the symptom or conflict causes distress, the relief it offers from a more threatening internal issue—like self-doubt or fear of failure—can make resolution feel dangerous rather than desirable.

Avoidance and externalization often operate alongside secondary gains, helping to maintain the narrative. By casting external circumstances as the root of her struggle, Calista could avoid acknowledging her own gaps in knowledge or skills. This reflects an external locus of control—the belief that one's outcomes are shaped by external forces rather than personal agency. While this stance can temporarily protect self-esteem, it ultimately undermines self-efficacy and stalls meaningful growth.

A reliance on secondary gains is often misunderstood as manipulation, but in clinical work, it's usually an unconscious psychological mechanism. It refers to any hidden benefit that sustains a problematic behavior or symptom. These benefits can include sympathy, attention, identity reinforcement, or, as in Calista's case, a reprieve from confronting a painful or threatening truth.

While confronting secondary gains can feel daunting at first, it's ultimately empowering: The path forward lies in helping the client become conscious of these gains and then finding healthier ways to achieve the same benefits. When clients understand what needs the maladaptive behavior is fulfilling, they can explore alternative strategies that serve those needs more constructively.

Confronting the secondary gains and finding better ways to meet her needs proved pivotal for Calista. With support, she was able to acknowledge that her core struggle was not interpersonal victimization but anxiety about her ability to meet her role's demands. Once she let go of the bullying narrative, she admitted to feeling overwhelmed by a few key aspects of her job—particularly in areas where she had never received formal training. This was difficult but liberating to admit.

Instead of focusing on interpersonal drama, Calista redirected her energy into addressing the actual problem. She enrolled in a series of weekend courses to boost her technical and organizational skills. Within a few months, her confidence improved dramatically—and so did her performance. Her stress levels decreased, and her relationships at work became more stable. She no longer needed to derive psychological safety from playing the victim's role because she had developed a more empowering source of security: competence.

By the end of our work together, Calista no longer used the word "bullying" to describe her experience. Instead, she spoke of "interpersonal tension," "skills gaps that I could fix with a few classes," and "performance anxiety"—terms that reflected clarity and personal responsibility. She had not only resolved the surface-level conflict but had restructured the way she interpreted and responded to stress at work.

This vignette illustrates a broader psychological truth: the secondary gains of victimhood can be deeply seductive, especially in environments that respond to victim narratives with attention and accommodation. But the resolution didn't lie in correcting a coworker's behavior or in changing company policy—it lay in Calista reclaiming her agency, strengthening her capabilities, and disentangling herself from a self-concept that no longer served her. Ultimately, what began as a protective distortion evolved into a point of transformation that was best for Calista and for the company.

Calista wasn't trying to wield victimhood as a tool to silence her opponent and win an argument; she just seemed to gravitate unconsciously toward victimhood as a strategy to avoid dealing directly with her issue of underperformance in the workplace. The harm she was causing to her colleague by formally accusing her of workplace bullying didn't even seem to register in Calista's awareness, although the stress of being investigated as a "bully" was undoubtedly a significant professional strain on the woman. But in other cases, labels like "bully" or "hate speech" can create a secondary gain of shielding the accuser from the need to engage in legitimate debate.

By definition, the term "bully" is reductive: it implies there is one "bad guy" who must be stopped and one innocent victim who should be supported.* Applying this moral framework to intellectual arguments is inherently stifling and ironically creates a dynamic in which the "bully" is typically rendered unable to speak. In addition to being reductive, the use of the term "bullying" in much of current parlance is inaccurate—by definition, a "bully" pertains to persistent antagonizing behavior toward a person who is virtually defenseless. The word "bully" conjures

---

* The word "bully" comes from sixteenth-century Dutch and originally connected a loving nickname; though its meaning has evolved to mean a strong person who persistently victimizes the weak. The word "victim" derives from Latin *victima*, and generally referred to an animal for religious sacrifice. The word "hate" has Germanic and Old English roots that connect to grief and treating one as an enemy.

an oversized tough high schooler stuffing a weak and defenseless puny little person into a locker. But when we're dealing with issues related to speech, in a society where threats of violence are punishable by law, using the word "bully" to describe an intellectual opponent is likely to be inaccurate at best and weaponizing at worst. What situations in life have you observed where terms like "hate speech" or "bully" are used to silence debate?

The final problem with shutting down "hate speech" is that there are certain things that we *should* hate or at least have a right to hate (serial killers, for example). What people or concepts are worthy of hatred, or even exactly how we *define* hatred can differ; to suggest banning *any hatred at all* is nonsensical and impractical. Some might suggest "banning" hatred of people based on immutable characteristics, but even this is problematic—as discussed earlier, I as a woman would much rather *know* a group's true feelings about women so that I could make fully informed decisions about how to navigate that group. Allowing people to hate is different from allowing them to commit violence against those they hate and/or to deprive the targets of their hatred of legal rights in society; forgetting this leads to chaos. As discussed in the "What about the need for *some* limits to free speech?" section coming next, we have laws prohibiting violence and certain types of discrimination in place; these laws allow us to have freedom of expression and a marketplace of ideas *without* endangering or depriving *anyone* of their rights to life, liberty, and the pursuit of happiness.

2. What about the need for *some* limits on free speech?

Another common objection to free speech is the logical (and correct!) assertion that truly unchecked freedom of speech would mean that slander and libel, along with threats of bodily harm or incitement to violence, would run rampant and cause great harm to society. As a clinical psychologist, I completely appreciate the concern, and it's important to remember that we have centuries of constitutional and legal precedent to attest that the vast majority of free speech advocacy is not about totally unchecked freedom of speech, Even those who do advocate for absolute freedom of speech are extremely unlikely to find success in our legal system. However, it's easy for this reassuring truth to get lost in the shuffle of a media cycle that revolves around the use of fear, anger, and terms like "constitutional crisis" to whip us up into a frenzy of clicks and doomscrolling. This is much easier for the media to do when we don't really understand what the current limits of free speech actually are.

Uncertainty typically increases anxiety, and without clear information it's easy to get caught in a "black-and-white thinking" trap where we feel forced to choose between a binary of repressive speech codes or a "Wild West" of unchecked free speech where even threats of actual violence will overrun our society. The good news is that our constitution and centuries of legal precedent offer a more nuanced approach than this binary choice. This book isn't a legal tome, but we will unpack some of the basic laws around speech as we address the question, "What about the need for *some* limits on speech?" It's important to share the basic ground rules about free speech to decrease uncertainty, and thereby decrease anxiety, about what exactly is meant by "free speech."

Another good reason to reduce uncertainty around the basic legal ground rules pertaining to free speech is that understanding boundaries can be a helpful way to manage or reduce feelings of anger. One of the healthy functions of anger is to motivate boundary-setting behaviors when an injustice has happened; when used appropriately, anger can help protect our rights, values, and well-being. For example, if someone maliciously mistreats you, your justifiable anger can galvanize you to take appropriate action to assert the proper boundaries (such as having a stern conversation and laying out consequences for what will happen if they continue to "cross you," or even hardening the boundary completely by ending the relationship). Depending on the situation, you would find an appropriate way to set the boundary of what you will allow into your life. When we have a clear sense of what the boundaries are, we are better equipped to regulate our emotions and engage in constructive discussions when we suspect a boundary has been violated. Clarity around rules and expectations makes it easier to find common ground with others, reducing unnecessary conflict.

Since anger is often linked to justice and boundary enforcement, it may help explain why social justice movements are often fueled by intense emotions and sometimes spin out into violence. Anger can be a natural and even a healthy response when people believe fundamental rights or moral principles are being violated. For those engaged in social justice activism, this likely feels like righteous anger, a justified and necessary reaction to perceived injustices. There are also people who simply like violence, and they may engage in what they call "social justice activism" as an excuse to act out violently. The natural role of anger when confronting injustice, and the connection for many between anger and violence, is another reason why it is crucial to avoid conflating disfavored speech with violence. When this conflation occurs, political violence can follow—such as in the case of the BLM riots of 2020, where $1–2 billion in property damages occurred and at least nineteen people were killed, or more recently the barrage of attacks on Tesla in response to Elon Musk's political involvement.[*]

---

[*]　As of April 2025, a spike in attacks on Teslas that began in January has spread over at least nine states, including Molotov cocktails and other forms of arson to set Teslas and dealerships ablaze, often accompanied by gunfire and graffiti such as "Nazi" or "Racist." Individual Tesla drivers have also been attacked during this recent spike, including at a parade in New Orleans where Tesla trucks were being used to transport materials. The vehicles were pelted with heavy objects till one of their glass tops cracked as protesters shouted "Nazi" and "F** Musk." Police escorts ultimately were needed in order for the vehicles to pass safely.

Now that we understand the psychological reasons why it's healthy to have a working knowledge of the basic ground rules of free speech, here are some helpful guideposts of the current legal environment for United States citizens. If you are subject to different laws or limits, I encourage you to learn about them for the reasons described above.

A. **Slander and libel are illegal.** Laws against saying or writing things that are factually false and could ruin a person's reputation were in place even before the US constitution was written. Because our legal system is based on English law, which began putting legal strictures against defamation in the thirteenth and fourteenth centuries, our constitution was never intended to allow for someone's reputation to be ruined by falsehoods. The *New York Times vs. Sullivan* (1964)[5] set higher bars for public figures to be defamed (such as demonstrating actual malice or reckless disregard for the truth).

B. **Incitement to violence and true threats of violence are illegal.** This is why the phrase "words are violence" bothers me so much as a psychologist—it is false, and it creates unnecessary anxiety as well as conflict escalation. While it's true that words can hurt, it's important to understand the difference between hurting feelings and hurting bodies. The metaphor, "His words were a slap in the face," is just that—a metaphor. It isn't literal. The point that words aren't actually violence should be too obvious to require much emphasis, but the sentiment behind the catchphrase "words are violence" has become a rallying cry to justify silencing speech and responding to speech with physical force, as if physical self-defense were warranted (see Google Trends—the phrase has gone from obscurity to peak popularity in recent years).[6]

C. **Fighting words are illegal.** Another category of speech that is not legally protected is something called "fighting words." This category of speech includes words that are intended as a direct personal insult so severe that it is likely to result in immediate violence. This category is extremely narrow. For example, the phrase "immediate violence" is quite literal—it is typically limited to speech that is face-to-face where violence could result immediately and directly before the victim has a moment to collect himself.[7] Courts will also consider if the context, such as whether the speech was delivered while physically breaching someone's space (e.g., delivering a personal insult while holding a fist in a "ready to strike" position inches away from the target's face, or putting one's face an inch from another's as you scream insults at him). To illustrate how narrow the scope of "fighting words" is, consider that an Ohio court determined in 2023 that a man who called his neighbor a "red-headed bitch"[8] to his face during a driveway dispute was not using fighting words, partly because the name-caller was on his own driveway while his neighbor was safely on his respective driveway, and the name-caller did not seem to be inviting any physical interaction. If the name-caller had crossed into his neighbor's driveway and violated his neighbor's physical space in an aggressive manner, his words may have become "fighting words."

For context about freedom of expression when it comes to topics that are often on the "cancel hotlist," it's important to note that laws prohibiting "fighting words" cannot be based on viewpoint discrimination, political affiliation, or union membership. The United States Supreme Court has also held that these laws also cannot exclusively target "race, color, creed, religion, or gender."[9] In other words, merely saying, "Trans women are actually men," or "Biological women should actually be called cis women" would almost certainly not qualify as "fighting words" because the speaker is merely stating a viewpoint, and it doesn't matter whether it's factually accurate. In cases like these, the law prioritizes the constitutional protection of speech, unless there is a direct incitement to actual, physical violence.

D. **Hate speech is not illegal**, and it is extremely difficult to define. While hate speech isn't illegal, it becomes illegal if it involves an actual threat of serious, imminent harm, as discussed above; or if it becomes targeted harassment (see the time, place, and manner restrictions). In other words, threats of violence and targeted harassment are illegal whether or not you have "hate in your heart." And since "hate" is subjective, there is more stability for everyone if laws are based on behavior rather than on feelings. While some might feel, at first blush, that it sounds appealing to simply outlaw anything "unkind" or "hateful," this strategy typically fosters the very result it is attempting to avoid. For example, hate speech against Jews in the Weimar Period of Germany was illegal, yet Hitler still rose to power. Many scholars[10] suggest that the laws against voicing perspectives like Hitler's actually facilitated the "forbidden fruit phenomena"[11] around them and ironically boosted the (originally underground) Nazi movement. This "taboo glamor" created an appeal for young and rebellious men, and of course the anti-speech laws made it extremely difficult to provide an effective counter message. There was literally no legal format to debate and debunk the worst parts of Hitler's insidious rhetoric, since a candid discussion was verboten. This meant the narrative was controlled primarily by those who were willing to break the law and gain power in the shadows, completely unchecked. For a more modern example, consider that the European Commission Against Racism and Intolerance found in 2024 that counter speech is a much more effective strategy against viewpoints that are typically defined as hate speech than simply making the speech illegal.[12] Strict speech codes don't really stop speech—they just force people to express or explore forbidden ideas in an underground manner, likely with fewer checks or challenges.

Daryl Davis is a striking example of the power of taking a pragmatic attitude toward hateful speech and greeting it with a counter message. A black R&B singer, Davis has converted dozens of former Ku Klux Klan members simply by engaging them in conversation. As Daryl Davis said in an interview with *The New York Times*, "If I can sit down and talk to K.K.K. members and neo-Nazis and get them to give me their robes and hoods and swastika flags and all that kind of crazy stuff, there's no reason why somebody can't sit down at a dinner table and talk to their family member."[13] Making words we dislike illegal is akin to a child on a playground covering her ears and screaming, "I can't hear you!" when the other children say something vexing, or not opening our credit card bills because we don't want to confront the debt. This primitive form of denial is actually one of the *least* effective ways of confronting problems.

The subjectivity of what constitutes "hate speech" is deepened by different members of various groups that could be targeted for "hatred" having different associations to certain words. For example, one person might find the phrase "cis woman" to be an offensive term because it implies that biological women are just a subcategory of an umbrella term, "woman" that includes trans-identifying biological males, and they might therefore label the term "cis woman" as misogynistic or hateful of women. On the other hand, another person might find the term "cis woman" an erudite way to be inclusive of trans-identified males who assert that failing to call them "trans women" is a denial of their humanity. Each side might view the other's linguistic choices as hateful, and therefore offensive, akin to a "four-letter word" (of course, the citizenry will also have wildly varying views on what constitutes a "four-letter word" and what their use represents in terms of sentiment). Ultimately, linguistic choices could be categorized as "taste and style" as referenced by Supreme Court Justice John Marshall Harlan in *Cohen vs. California* (1971):[14]

"While the particular four-letter word being litigated here is perhaps more distasteful than most others of its genre, it is nevertheless often true that one man's vulgarity is another's lyric. Indeed, we think it is largely because governmental officials cannot make principled distinctions in this area that the Constitution leaves matters of taste and style so largely to the individual."

Since the labels we use to describe one another are ultimately about taste and style choices that reflect our opinions, allowing the government to selectively ban speech as "hateful" is fraught with an inherent unfairness. Why should the government decide whose speech is acceptable, and thereby privilege one group's taste and style over another's? Especially in a democratic republic such as the United States where the government leadership is elected by a majority of voters, such a strategy would intrinsically fail to protect the minority. Political candidates would promote speech codes that pandered to whichever groups were most populous or politically active; it would essentially amount to the use of mob rule to control speech. As a reminder, protecting the right of citizenry to express themselves according to their own "taste and style" does not protect speech that incites others to violence. But outside of these areas (and other limited carve-outs for speech intended to commit fraud, perjury, or other crimes) it does allow the citizenry to choose their own words to express their beliefs.

E. **Free speech under the First Amendment does allow for "time, place, and manner" restrictions**. This means that while it is perfectly legal to utter the words, "Women are stupid," a city could legally deny a demonstration permit where the intention was to blast this message through loudspeakers directly outside of a Girl Scouts meeting. Such a scenario would likely constitute targeted harassment, which is different from having a spirited dinner discussion or an organized debate where the merits (or lack thereof) of this idea could be explored and exposed. In a similar sense, Florida's controversial Parental Rights in Education Act was dubbed as the "don't say gay" bill by detractors who said the bill squashed the free speech rights of teachers. However, this bill was actually a "time place and manner" restriction because it simply prohibited teachers from discussing sexuality (including their own) with schoolchildren in grades kindergarten through third grade during the course of their work as teachers. Teachers, along with the rest of Florida citizens, are welcome to discuss their sexuality in other places, including the public square.

One striking way to clarify the meaning of a "time, place, and manner" restriction is to contrast it with an actual example of a "public square" restriction. Consider that Twitter disallowed making the assertion that "trans women are actually men" on its platform, even though Twitter enjoys Section 230 benefits as a semipublic space,

or a "public square." This would be tantamount to saying
that Florida citizens cannot discuss their sexuality anywhere in the public square. Obviously this is quite different than a time, place, and manner restriction where
teachers are welcome to discuss their sexuality however
they wish in their private lives and even their public lives,
but just not in the specific situation of being on the job
teaching schoolchildren.

F. **Internet as public utility**. At times, the FCC has considered the internet as a public utility, and places like X (formerly Twitter) are often considered to function as a public
square. Again, this book is not a legal tome, but a basic
understanding of our speech laws may help to contain
the anxiety and concern felt by some around free speech
online. Platforms like Google, Facebook, and X are protected by something called Section 230. Section 230 is a
governmental protection from the 1996 Communications
Decency Act that gives special benefits to these companies in exchange for these companies recognizing themselves as being open for use by the public (similar to
old-fashioned telephone lines having the benefit of being
placed on public lands for the greater good). In other
words, just like the phone company isn't responsible for
what you say on the phone, and it would be absurd for
the phone company to attempt to control what you say
on the phone, Section 230–protected online platforms are
open public forums that receive special government protections that absolve them from general responsibility for
what individual users may say. They are different from a
newspaper platform where the private publisher has editorial power to curate the content but also bears legal
responsibility for their choices. On Section 230–protected
platforms, the public is supposed to be free to speak as if

it's a public square, even if someone else considers their words "hateful." Of course, prohibitions against violence and threats of violence are illegal no matter where or how they are made, but the words must syntactically signal a threat of violence, not merely be unkind or unpopular words that metaphorically feel like "a slap in the face." It's also important to remember that we don't have to expose ourselves to everything online, just like we don't have to read every book that exists. We can and should curate our media diet. Many platforms make it easy to adjust your personal account settings so that you'll never even see posts or comments with whatever words or topics you wish to avoid. Living in a society that recognizes a right to free speech doesn't mean you can't have boundaries. A free speech society such as the United States simply recognizes the intelligence and discernment of its citizenry and empowers them to decide for themselves what speech they will hear (with caveats for threats of violence and similar cases of course).

Free speech often raises boundary questions. Where does one person's right to express themselves end, and where do the rights of others begin? Without clear guidelines, discussions around speech can quickly become emotionally charged and divisive. However, when we establish a shared understanding of legal boundaries, we create a framework that can have a calming and unifying effect. Even if you disagree with current legal standards and predominant legislative perspectives, at least understanding the ground rules empowers you to work on acceptance, build bridges, and possibly engage in advocacy from an informed position.

Now that we've reduced uncertainty by covering the basic ground rules of what "free speech" really means in our current society (at least in the United States), you can work on accepting the boundaries and learning to work within them or perhaps work toward changing them if you feel strongly that you see something problematic within our current legal framework. The good news is that, like anger, anxiety also has a healthy function: it stimulates preparation behaviors. If you feel frustrated or anxious about free speech issues in your community, consider channeling that energy into civic involvement. Engaging in local discussions, supporting organizations that align with your values, or advocating for legislative change can provide a sense of agency and turn emotional distress into productive action.

Vignette: Courtney's Fear of Words

Courtney was a vivacious middle-aged woman who had long struggled with obsessive-compulsive disorder—this time centered around fears of saying the wrong thing to her close-knit group of girlfriends. She was terrified of expressing the wrong opinion or being exposed to "the wrong ideas." Over the years, she had seen how people in her social and professional circles could be quietly or publicly ostracized for expressing dissenting political views, and she was horrified by the possibility of the same thing happening to her.

The issue came to a head when one of the women started a group text thread in response to the overturning of *Roe v. Wade* (1973).[15] The thread centered around ways to join protest efforts—such as attending rallies, contacting state representatives, or donating to abortion-care resources—and was written with the assumption that everyone in the group would see the issue the same way.

Courtney had once viewed the topic in similar black-and-white terms. But not long before that, a video had popped up on her social media of a doctor speaking calmly about the ethical case for placing term limits on abortion. She clicked on it without thinking much of it but found herself surprised by how reasonable the speaker sounded. She didn't agree with everything he said, but she couldn't easily dismiss it either. She had expected outrage; what she encountered was nuance. Something in her shifted.

After that, her social media algorithm began serving her similar videos: interviews with adults who had survived failed abortion attempts, former abortion providers sharing their journeys to viewing abortion differently, and quiet, reflective conversations about the moral complexity surrounding the issue. She felt almost powerless to resist watching them. She hadn't gone looking for this content, but now that it had found her, she couldn't look away. Her previously rigid view of abortion had begun to soften.

She was irritated that this problematic new perspective had "gotten in her head" and soon became paralyzed by the fear that she might accidentally "out herself" by saying something to reveal the "stain" of her evolving viewpoint. She originally sought therapy to expunge these "bad ideas," but no amount of reading or arguing with herself could undo the shift. In fact, the more she learned, the more her perspective evolved, rather than retreating. Instead of focusing on eradicating her burgeoning awareness, our sessions focused on accepting and exploring it; and considering how she might integrate her whole, authentic self with her friend group.

As her thinking moved further from what she imagined to be the group consensus, her anger and fear intensified. She was angry with herself, and even angry at the videos—she knew it was irrational to blame a video, but a part of her held them responsible for "infecting" her with a perspective that now felt like a liability.

Courtney was also deeply concerned that if she surrendered to her newfound heterodox views, she would need to cut off contact with her friends—or, more accurately, that they would cut off contact with her. But she eventually discovered that the road to wellness was not found in purging herself of unpopular ideas or clinging to fragile friendships, but in learning to tolerate diverse viewpoints and build relationships with people willing to do the same.

She developed her ability to discern when and how to disclose sensitive viewpoint information by learning techniques like WAIT (featured in part 2 of this book) and she practiced mindfulness exercises to foster a healthy detachment from her thoughts. Eventually, she was able to share her new views judiciously with the group. As she feared, a couple of them reacted with vitriol, accused her of misogyny, and cut off contact. But to her surprise, most of the group was more accepting than she had given them credit for—and one friend even confided that she, too, had recently begun to reevaluate the issue.

Courtney came to understand that her identity is not fused with her ideas—and that honest thinking and meaningful connection are both possible, even amid cultural polarization.

3. What about misinformation?

Another common and well-intentioned objection to free speech often involves issues around "misinformation." Google Trends show that interest in this word spiked around February 2020, and has remained elevated even years after the pandemic ended. While ensuring a high level of quality about the information we receive is certainly a sensible goal, limiting open dialogue is not the best way to achieve it. Here are some factors to weigh against the assertion that stifling free speech will somehow improve the quality of information in our everyday lives:

1. Libel, slander, and fraud are already illegal, so some legal and objective limits on misinformation are already in place. Just like free speech doesn't include latitude to make threats of violence, it also includes some protections about accuracy. However, free speech generally empowers the public to evaluate written or spoken material and decide for themselves whether they believe it wholly, partially, or not at all—and they're free to change their minds with the passing of time or the introduction of further information. There is no "Ministry of Truth" or "Big Brother" as an arbiter for the public, à la George Orwell's dystopian novel *1984*.

2. Experts and authorities are often wrong. This has been true historically as well as recently. Here are a few examples to ponder as we consider the possibility of what might happen if the government, church, academia, or some other body (however well-intentioned they may be) were to have decision power over what types of conversations or debates can be had by the public:

   a. Galileo was actually placed under house arrest for the rest of his life as a result of his heretical talk suggesting the Earth orbits the sun. All the authorities of his time believed the "science was settled" on the sun orbiting the Earth. Today, we all understand that he was actually correct.

   b. Intelligence of Women: In 1873, Dr. Edward H. Clarke, a Harvard Medical School professor, published *Sex in Education; or, A Fair Chance for Girls*, arguing that rigorous education for women could harm their reproductive health and, implicitly, their intellectual capacity, as their brains were supposedly less suited for sustained effort. In 1925, Sigmund Freud wrote, "Some Psychological Consequences of the Anatomical Distinction Between the Sexes," which indicated that women's intellectual development was shaped by "penis envy," implying a psychological handicap. Freud was widely accepted at the time and grew in popularity for decades to come.

c. Lobotomies were once considered a valid form of health care. Rosemary Kennedy, the sister of future president John F. Kennedy, had one in 1941. In fact, Portuguese neurologist António Egas Moniz won the 1949 Nobel Prize in Physiology or Medicine for inventing the leucotomy, which involved drilling holes into the skull to sever connections in the prefrontal cortex.

d. In the 1950s and 1960s, tobacco companies often featured medical doctors assuring the public that cigarettes were safe, and even sometimes recommended them as aids for digestion or stress; they often cited industry-funded research. They even indicated cigarettes were safe during pregnancy. Even decades later in 1994, tobacco executives testified under oath before congress that nicotine was not addictive.

e. In the 2020s, the COVID-19 pandemic revealed how, even today, well-meaning experts can misjudge critical medical issues. Lockdowns and widespread masking, even of young children, were initially endorsed by experts as the only way to avert millions of deaths. These assertions were supported by alarming predictive models, yet later studies, including the Johns Hopkins meta-analysis[*] and Sweden's lighter approach,[**] showed they barely reduced mortality while triggering massive economic and social harm. The lab-leak theory, once ridiculed by experts and media as a fringe conspiracy, was dismissed in favor of a natural origin, but years later, intelligence reports and scientific scrutiny exposed it as a highly plausible scenario. (As of this writing, there is no definitive answer on the origins.)

Similarly, the safety and efficacy of the mRNA COVID-19 vaccine were initially presented with

---

[*]   A meta-analysis conducted by researchers at Johns Hopkins University, published in January 2022, reviewed twenty-four studies to assess the impact of lockdowns on COVID-19 mortality. The study concluded that lockdowns in Europe and the United States reduced COVID-19 mortality by an average of only 0.2 percent. The authors stated that while lockdowns had little to no public health effects, they imposed enormous economic and social costs where they were adopted.

Jonas Herby, Lars Jonung, and Steve H. Hanke, *A Literature Review and Meta-Analysis of the Effects of Lockdowns on COVID-19 Mortality*, Studies in Applied Economics No. 200 (Baltimore, MD: Johns Hopkins Institute for Applied Economics, Global Health, and the Study of Business Enterprise, 2022). https://sites.krieger.jhu.edu/iae/files/2022/01/A-Literature-Review -and-Meta-Analysis-of-the-Effects-of-Lockdowns-on-COVID-19 -Mortality.pdf.

[**]   Sweden adopted a less restrictive approach during the COVID-19 pandemic, avoiding strict lockdowns and keeping schools open. A study published in *Frontiers in Public Health* in 2023 reported that Sweden's excess mortality rate was 158 per 100,000, ranking 37th among 42 countries, and not significantly different from its Nordic neighbors: Norway (129), Denmark (97), and Finland (228). This suggests that Sweden's lighter approach did not result in substantially higher mortality compared to countries with stricter measures.

Anders Björkman, Magnus Gisslén, Martin Gullberg, and Johnny Ludvigsson, "The Swedish COVID-19 Approach: A Scientific Dialogue on Mitigation Policies," *Frontiers in Public Health* 11 (2023): 1206732, https: //doi.org/10.3389/fpubh.2023.1206732.

expert assurances of near-perfection, but the experts missed or glossed over the fact that the virus would still be transmissible and natural immunity provided comparable if not superior protection. The vaccine also carried rare but real risks like myocarditis, autoimmune issues, and menstrual cycle changes. Mounting data eventually made these problems impossible to ignore. Meanwhile, dissenting voices were censored. For example, Dr. Robert Malone, a Harvard Medical School trained physician and prestigious scientist renowned for his pioneering work on mRNA vaccine technology, was suspended from Twitter for his discussion of the COVID-19 vaccine. Similarly, Dr. Jay Bhattacharya, a Stanford professor at the time, is now known to have been placed on a then-secret blacklist by Twitter that was designed to limit the visibility of accounts that questioned the wisdom of COVID-19 lockdown policies, which he did. Dr. Bhattacharya has now been confirmed by the United States Senate as the director of the National Institutes of Health, and the harms of lockdown policies (educational losses, mental health issues, and more) are well documented.[16, 17]

These are not all cases of outright censorship, but they do illustrate that depriving people of information and open discussion limits our ability to transmit information, engage in spirited debate, and have intellectual autonomy. Since we can't rely on "experts" to always be right (it would be unfair to the experts if we had this expectation), we must be able to think and speak for ourselves. This doesn't mean we disregard experts; we should be free to read studies and discuss or debate them ourselves, or watch various experts present their viewpoints and then decide for ourselves who seems more credible. Or we can opt out—we don't have to participate in every debate, but stifling certain experts and favoring others only hampers the quality of information that's readily available to those who want to do a deep intellectual dive into whatever topic they wish. The free marketplace of ideas is a better tool to combat misinformation than allowing centralized sources to exercise top-down power to squash or throttle voices that question science that is supposedly "settled."

When we don't allow open debate, we become vulnerable to self-censorship, outright censorship, the illusion of unanimity, and other conditions outlined in chapter 3 that contribute to the rise of groupthink.

Vignette on the Dangers of Groupthink

A pair of loving, intelligent parents living in New York City—surrounded by some of the most prestigious hospitals and specialists in the world—found themselves swept into a rising tide of clinical and familial pressure. Their adolescent daughter had become distressed about her gender, and the professionals they turned to, from therapists to pediatric endocrinologists, all seemed to speak with one voice. Every expert insisted that the "best practices," the "only ethical approach," was to affirm their daughter's identity as a boy and begin medical interventions as soon as possible. Puberty blockers. Testosterone. Chest surgery. These were presented not as options, but as necessities. To hesitate was to risk being labeled abusive, unloving, or dangerously uninformed.

And yet . . . something didn't sit right with them. Despite the confident assurances from white coats and academic titles, the parents couldn't shake a nagging feeling that what they were being told simply didn't make sense. Could a girl truly become a boy? Was halting puberty and altering her body really the best path forward for their daughter's well-being—or was this a situation of blind conformity dressed up as medical consensus? That's when they reached out to me.

Our phone call was not just a consultation; it was, in their words, a moment of awakening. I listened to their story, validated their concerns, and gently questioned the dominant narrative they had been told. I sent them research, including the Cass Review[18] out of the United Kingdom (UK), which had raised serious questions about the long-term safety and efficacy of medicalizing gen-der-distressed youth. We discussed the limitations of the evidence base for these treatments, the growing interna-tional trend toward caution, and the fact that respected medical bodies in Sweden,[19] Finland,[20] Norway,[21] and the UK[22] had begun pulling back on these interventions for minors[23] and had voiced concern, pointedly questioning the quality of the research used to justify these surgeries and making clear that they disagreed with the existence of "medical consensus"[24] in favor of performing them on minors. These studies affirmed to the parents that they were not alone in their doubts.

They told me afterward that our conversation felt like breathing fresh air after being stuck in a sealed room. For the first time in months, someone had acknowledged the unease they'd felt but had been too intimidated to voice. I hadn't told them what to do—I had simply reminded them that critical thinking was not cruelty, and that true love for a child involves asking hard questions, even when everyone around you is shouting for you not to.

Two years later, their daughter is doing much better. She no longer identifies as male and has grown into a deeper understanding of herself, supported by parents who chose to pause and reflect rather than follow the crowd. Her body is intact. Her voice remains her own. And though adolescence was not easy, she is now in a much stronger place emotionally and mentally, without having undergone irreversible interventions.

The parents reached out later to tell me how often they reflect on that pivotal moment with gratitude—how that one phone call helped them resist the illusion of unanimity that lies at the heart of groupthink. At the time, they felt utterly alone, but now they know they were part of a much larger wave of families, clinicians, and researchers who have since dared to question. The United States Department of Health and Human Services has now joined much of Europe and acknowledged the real risks associated with medical transition for minors. What once seemed like fringe skepticism is now part of the public conversation.

Looking back, these parents say they were dangerously close to making a decision that might have led to one of their greatest regrets. They are not anti-trans. They are not anti-science. They are simply grateful they had the courage—and the support—to step outside the echo chamber long enough to see clearly. In a culture where dissent is often punished and conformity is mistaken for compassion, the courage to ask, "But what if this isn't true?"—and to say it out loud—can be all it takes to pierce the illusion of unanimity and break the spell of groupthink.

PART TWO
Tools for Open Dialogue

**Courage is what it takes to stand up and speak; courage
is also what it takes to sit down and listen.**
—WINSTON CHURCHILL

Now that you've learned about the value of open dialogue, here
are some tools to facilitate it. You might be surprised to see that
some of the tools actually involve learning to hold your tongue,
and how to extricate yourself if you decide you *don't* want to be in
dialogue with someone. Why would those tools be included here
if speaking up is so good for us? The reason is that when we're
seeking *open dialogue*. We don't want to speak *compulsively*, just
openly. Open dialogue doesn't mean we have to *share everything*
with everyone all the time, and it doesn't mean have to *listen* to
anything and everything that comes our way. Healthy boundaries
are partly what make sharing and listening meaningful.

While there are true introverts and extroverts, many of us
are actually a combination of the two depending on the situation. This is why we may sometimes find it hard to speak up,
and other times have a hard time *shutting* up. There's a time and
a place for both. Understanding the difference between healthy

self-restraint and self-censorship will make it easier to choose the right tools for any situation.

Healthy Self-Restraint

Self-restraint can connote a healthy self-awareness and consideration of others. For example, the workplace is sometimes a "caution zone" where it's wise to moderate how much we share about *any* topic from our personal life. This isn't the case in *all* workplaces, of course, but workplaces are just a common example of where a person might limit sharing about sensitive subjects out of a desire to keep the primary focus on work.

Similarly, a student beginning a new semester might keep their sociopolitical views close to the vest. Some college students aren't worried about ideological clashes with their peers or professors, but many feel differently.[1] And due to the halo effect,[2] we're often known by the first impression we make. So while jumping into a charged classroom discussion early in the semester may be fine for some, it's understandably avoided by many. We may also want to restrain ourselves from speaking so that we can *listen* more actively to others' viewpoints in order to be better informed, to draw out a shy person, to show deference in appropriate situations, or to help our loved ones to feel truly heard we're often known by the first impression we make. So while jumping into a charged classroom discussion early in the semester may be fine for some, it's understandably avoided by many. We may also want to restrain ourselves from speaking so that we can *listen* more actively to others' viewpoints in order to be better informed, to draw out a shy person, to show deference in appropriate situations, or to help our loved ones to feel truly heard.

The examples above are ones I would put in the "healthy self-restraint" category. Being judicious and mindful about sharing certain viewpoints can actually be a prosocial behavior that demonstrates the virtue of self-control. Being a good listener can also, ironically, help people to hear *you* better. When people feel that you're listening generously, giving them "airtime," and seeking to *understand* rather than *correct* them, they will often become more receptive to listening to you as well. However, if you find yourself *always* holding back, or feeling as if too many people in your life don't really know you, especially in your personal life, then you might be self-censoring.

Self-Censorship

The root of the word "censor" traces back to the Roman magistrates in the fifth century BCE. They would take the census and simultaneously inform the citizenry which moral viewpoints were currently acceptable. The citizens had to comply with whatever the censors decreed—in other words, they had to live as if a censor were following them around, permanently within earshot, and ensure that their words and deeds conformed to whatever viewpoints had been mandated. For the purpose of this book, we'll define self-censoring as more than just holding your tongue on certain occasions, which can be healthy (as we'll see). Self-censoring is acting as if a modern version of the Roman censors decide which viewpoints are acceptable, and then habitually stifling or hiding your true views on topics that are important to you in order to adhere to those "censors." You may censor yourself to the point where you may eventually feel like people don't know the "real you," or you start feeling disconnected from your actual thoughts because you know they are "verboten" in the places where you spend a lot of your time.

Self-censorship is feeling the need to keep your views *secret* rather than *private*. The difference between secrecy and privacy is often that secrecy is marked by a *fear* that if the secret were discovered, an undesirable consequence or outcome would arise (e.g., the professor would lower your grade, your aunt would alienate you, your friend group would delink with you on social media, or you'd get metaphorically uninvited to the company barbecue). Secrecy is often the motivation for suppression—when a thought arises during conversation that seems like a logical and meaningful remark, but you feel a strong impulse to stuff it down and *hide* it. Sometimes, it's easier just to pretend to hold others' views so that we can "go along and get along." If we do this often enough, we can start to repress our thoughts and potentially interrupt the cognitive, social and emotional gifts of language discussed in part 1.

The tools in part 2 are broken into two general categories: Speaking up and Self-restraint. There's a time and a place for both. I'm not here to tell you *when* to speak up or exercise self-restraint; I want you to feel equipped to do whichever you feel is *healthiest* for you in any situation.

Feel free to think of the tools here like recipes in a cookbook: they don't need to be used in order, they can be used according to your needs in any given situation. As a reminder, I'd love to hear from you about how these tools or any of the other approaches in this book work in your life—and if you have any techniques of your own to add, I'm all ears!

Chapter 5

Seven Tools for Speaking Up

Our lives begin to end the day we become silent about things that matter.
—COMMONLY ATTRIBUTED TO MARTIN LUTHER KING JR.

When you've decided it's time to speak up, feel free to dive in and do so—sometimes it can be very liberating. On the other hand, if you feel nervous about taking the plunge, remember that the healthy function of anxiety is to stimulate preparation behaviors— that was the whole point of my previous book, *Nervous Energy: Harness the Power of Your Anxiety.* The tools in this chapter are to help you channel anxiety about speaking up into a constructive, thoughtful plan of action. Don't do yourself the disservice of assuming that anxiety is an automatic "stop sign." Oftentimes, anxiety just means that you have a realistic and healthy awareness of potential pitfalls, and that awareness can be a gift that guides you to make a few simple preparations to set yourself up for success. The tools below cover a wide variety of circumstances, including an option for what to do if speaking up in a direct manner is truly ill-advised.

1. Reflective Listening

This technique from couples therapy is typically used to help couples work through heated disagreements. While it's located in the Speaking Up toolbox, it can actually help you to speak up *and* to be a better listener. It's a structured exercise that ensures each person has a chance to say their piece, and that both parties are truly *understanding each other*. The structured time-based format removes the issue of "fighting for airtime," which helps decrease tension because being verbally interrupted at the wrong time can escalate arguments quickly. The exercise's component of summarizing the other's viewpoints helps slow down our thought process to facilitate deeper thinking around important topics and helps us develop new perspectives when appropriate. The format also ensures both parties are *understanding* one another—many arguments have escalated due to both parties "talking past each other," oftentimes completely misunderstanding what the other party is even actually saying. This exercise can be good to suggest to others if you want reassurance of a relatively peaceful dialogue when sharing a viewpoint the other person might be quick to label or dismiss; and it can be helpful if you'd like to invite a reticent person in your life to engage in meaningful dialogue about sensitive topics.

Step 1: Start by choosing a partner. Explain in advance that the first person will make a short point (no more than one minute long*) and then the second person will simply repeat the point

---

* It is essential that the speaker doesn't talk more than a minute at a time, otherwise it can be very hard for the listener to accurately recapitulate the point. There's no shame in using a timer if it's helpful. Some people like a timer because it helps them develop self-awareness about how much they're asking the other person to comprehend at once; and other people like it because it encourages them to speak a little longer than they normally might. The timer can also help everyone stay calmer as it neutralizes any sense of having to compete for space in the conversation (feeling interrupted or verbally cut off during a disagreement can heighten power struggles or other tensions).

back to the best of their ability. The second person will make sure to use a calm, rational tone that conveys respect and/or compassion for the person who spoke first—despite potentially disagreeing with whatever they said. If you're the person suggesting this exercise, I recommend letting your partner decide who will share first.

Step 2: Repeat step 1 until the first speaker confirms their point was correctly understood. Sometimes this happens on the first attempt, but sometimes it takes a few tries. If it takes a few tries, don't get discouraged—this means it's a good thing you're doing this exercise, since you're skillfully avoiding the common pitfall of "talking past each other" by arguing without even truly understanding each other. Each time you and your partner reattempt step 2, you're showing the other person that they matter enough for you to speak and listen with care.

Step 3: Next, the speaker and the listener switch roles and repeat the exercise—this time the new speaker makes his or her own independent point or reaction to be recapitulated by the new listener. For the listener, it can be helpful to take in a slow deep breath while you listen—but no need to do this if you're already feeling relaxed.

Step 4: Keep repeating steps 1–3 until both sides feel understood.

Helpful hint: The goal is not necessarily to agree, but to increase understanding of what the other person thinks or feels and why they hold that position. The structure of this exercise accounts for the presence of what psychologists call "hot cognition," which is cognition that is heavily influenced by our emotional state. In contrast, "cold cognition" describes a thought process that is purely rational and geared toward processing information. By slowing down to summarize what the other person has said, we "cool our cognition" by forcing our mind to focus more on the information they've provided. This might be especially important to do with political topics: Researchers at the State University of New York at Stony Brook[1] found that when we are exposed to a political concept about which we already have a strong emotional position, brain activity arises to reflect that particular emotional state at the mere mention of the political topic. This means that if we feel hostile or angry about certain political topics, we may need help to manage our initial emotional reactions and remain coolheaded enough to have productive conversations about those topics. Reflective listening helps with this, because focusing on understanding each other on a factual level nudges us into a cooler, information-processing form of cognition when we might otherwise be pulled into hot cognition based on our preconceived notions about the topic (or about people who hold certain positions on said topic). Even if our preconceived notions turn out to be correct, remaining calm and factual will still help to facilitate better dialogue.

If you're in a situation where you think Reflective Listening would help but it feels awkward to suggest, you have a few choices:

- Try inviting the person to do the exercise anyway. Sometimes, people may surprise you by being more open-minded than you think. You can even work it into the conversation naturally by explaining how you came to be interested in this technique by saying, "I read this book by a psychologist and she mentioned an exercise that can be helpful when people are discussing emotional topics. It seemed interesting, do you want to try it?" (You can also say "passionate" if you think the person might bristle at the word "emotional.")
- You can "back your way into" the technique without formally introducing it. Start by listening carefully and

repeating back what the other person said, explaining that you just want to be sure you understood them correctly. Next, you can ask them if they'd like to hear what you think about the topic. If they say yes, their verbal commitment will help them to mentally accept that they currently have a role of being a listener. Go ahead and say your piece, and conclude by saying, "I'd love to hear your response, but first if you don't mind just telling me what you heard me say, I just want to make sure I communicated clearly."

If they respond negatively to your question about whether they'd like to hear your position, at least you've gotten them to own the fact that they are not open to hearing other viewpoints. Although you didn't get to speak up in the way you intended, you made a very powerful point by putting this person's stone wall tactic into stark relief. Depending on the relationship, you can decide the best way to respond: If it's a coworker, perhaps you just want to distance yourself from building a personal relationship with someone who clearly views conversations in a one-sided manner. If it's your spouse, you might wait for things to calm down and then approach them to inquire about how they felt when you listened to them; and ask gently about why they don't want to extend the same level of openness to hearing your views.

- Try other techniques listed here to build rapport, and keep an eye out for another time when it feels more comfortable to invite them to try Reflective Listening.

2. Make a Clear Plan for a Clear Head

If you feel piqued with anxiety when speaking up in certain situations, you might experience a temporary dip in your ability to think creatively and rationally in those moments. This is a holdover from our caveman days: When we encountered a threat (e.g., a rattlesnake), we did *not* want to waste any cognitive energy on nonessential tasks like personal reflection or nuanced relationship skills, so our brain paused any nonessential thought streams so that we could focus like a laser beam on the threat. This "shutdown system" is helpful in life-and-death danger situations, but unhelpful in most of our everyday life—especially if we're entering into an intellectually or emotionally challenging conversation where we want to present our views in a bold-yet-thoughtful manner, preserve or enrich our relationships, and respond nimbly to those who disagree (or who may even try to shut us down).

To protect against a "brain freeze" during what you anticipate will be a charged conversation, it can be helpful to stop and make a plan *before* you speak up. This is a similar strategy to making an exit plan for fire safety: We calmly map out the best strategy (which is often very obvious when we're not in a panic) so that we won't freeze when things get hectic. For some of us, speaking up can feel like we're entering a metaphorical fire—especially if we're thinking of speaking up to a professor, an overbearing-but-powerful relative, or some other person in a position of authority who uses their power to shut down or intimidate diverse viewpoints. While these situations are particularly grating because we *know* they're coming and feel as if we're just "waiting for the other shoe to drop," one positive is that their *predictability* can *empower* us to make a plan—and *good* plans can help to decrease anxiety as well as improve outcomes.

There is no one-size-fits-all plan since every situation is different, but here are some building blocks to decrease anxiety and put your best foot forward in ongoing (and therefore predictable) situations where speaking up requires courage:

Seven Building Blocks for a Clear Plan

I. Find an ally: Speaking up alone is generally much harder compared to when you have an ally. From an evolutionary perspective, we feel safety in numbers; we're more vulnerable when we're alone. One of the first things a bully does is to isolate the victim, but the target having an ally makes it harder. Plus, having a buddy can be a stress reliever. So, if you're thinking of speaking up in a classroom, meeting, or a family gathering where your viewpoint is typically ostracized, it can be helpful to consider having an ally who agrees to back you up. Knowing that at least *someone* else will say, "Yes, I feel the same way sometimes—I think she has a point!" can make all the difference. Consider confiding in someone that you're planning to speak up and ask if they'd agree to back you up when the time comes.

II. Write your points down: If you're speaking up in a situation where you are likely to get strong pushback or where the stakes are high, it can be helpful to list your points in advance along with your response to any counterpoints you anticipate. You may even want to jot down a few facts or statistics that support your perspective, potentially along with a quote or two from an academic or company policy handbook, if relevant. Whether or not you refer to your notes in the conversation is up to you—glancing at your notes may be perfectly normal in classroom discussions or workplace meetings, but it might seem out of place in more casual settings. If using your notes in the conversation doesn't feel natural, consider using your notes to prepare a mental acronym that will help you remember your main points if things get heated. A memory aid like an acronym can help to reduce the cognitive load of trying to remember your points while also processing what the other person has said, and it can be a soothing road map to keep you on track with the points you wanted to make if you are prone to "brain freezes" during moments of anxiety. The acronym can also serve as a mental touchstone that helps you to feel calm by serving as a reminder of the careful preparation you've done for this conversation. Even if you choose to forgo an acronym as well as taking any written notes to the conversation, the exercise of listing your points, along with responses to anticipated counterpoints, can bolster your feeling of preparedness and help protect against the cognitive "system shutdown" that sometimes occurs during moments of real or perceived threat. These preparations will help on a logistical *and* an emotional level to decrease the chances of frustrating post-conversation thoughts like, "Oh! I should have said . . ."

III. Say your line: When we feel especially anxious about initiating what we anticipate might be a difficult conversation, taking that first step—the opening line—can feel daunting. Often, the hardest part is simply beginning. In these moments, it can be helpful to depersonalize the situation. One effective way to do this is to imagine yourself as an actor, whose only task is to deliver a line or two as part of a script.

This mental shift can make it easier to take a deep breath, open your mouth, and say what needs to be said. For example, you might start with something as simple as, "Actually, I see it differently. Would you like to know why?"

This approach is rooted in a cognitive behavioral therapy technique called *cognitive rehearsal*, in which individuals envision challenging scenarios and how they'll handle them as a form of preparation for the actual event. Just as actors rehearse scenes and memorize their lines, you too can mentally practice your opening statement—or any specific point you anticipate will be difficult to express—so that, when the moment comes, you can simply "perform" the line.

A word of caution: While you can rehearse detailed scenarios in your mind, it's important to remember that you can't predict exactly how others will respond. Moreover, maintaining a depersonalized, performative stance throughout an entire conversation has limitations and could come across as emotionally distant. That's why I recommend using the role-play technique in this chapter if you want to build deeper, authentic comfort with more complex conversational dynamics. But for a quick shot of courage—especially when you need to say just one or two important sentences—the "say your line" method can be a powerful tool.

One more caveat: As I discussed in my previous book, *Nervous Energy: Harness the Power of Your Anxiety*, the healthy function of anxiety is to stimulate preparation. If you have a great deal of anxiety about starting a conversation or saying a particular thing, use your anxiety as a signal to pause and reflect: Is there additional preparation you need to do before initiating the conversation? Talking with a trusted friend or advisor, or trying the WAIT technique detailed in this chapter, can help you determine whether your anxiety is pointing to additional reflection preparation.

Once you've done the necessary preparation and feel confident that you're ready—aside from a few jitters about one or two phrases—the "say your line" technique can provide just the nudge you need to dive in.

IV. Consider your timing: The best timing will depend on the person you're approaching, as well as your goal—in some cases, you *want* to speak up in front of others for the sake of a rational group discussion, or to create a more open social atmosphere. Remember the Asch line experiment, where participants actually misstated obvious information about line lengths, simply because everyone else did so?* Your goal might be to help "break the spell" of groupthink and deliberately bring diversity to an otherwise homogeneous conversation. On the other hand, people are often more receptive to criticism if it is presented in private, so there are advantages to finding a quiet, private place as well and confiding to your manager or a "social ringleader" that you sometimes feel stifled. Sometimes, a combination might be best—you could approach the person in private to explain that sometimes you feel shut down and hopefully get their assurance that your viewpoint is welcome. Then *that* person could actually become your ally when you voice your perspective in a group discussion.

V. Arm yourself with information: In some situations, especially professional or academic settings, it's helpful to understand the parameters of how speaking up could affect your position at the institution. For example, are you raising an issue merely to assert your preferences of how you *wish* things were run, or is it really a matter of your legal rights? Does your school or employer have a handbook that outlines policies that might affect your current situation, and are those policies being applied correctly? If you aren't sure of the answer to these questions, consider reviewing appropriate handbooks or talking to a lawyer

---

* This is explained in part 1, but basically the Asch study is a classic psychology study that demonstrated how easy it is to get people to say things that aren't true simply by surrounding them with others who are saying the untrue thing. The study involved getting participants in a psychology study to say that one line was shorter than the other, when this was obviously incorrect. Solomon E. Asch, "Opinions and Social Pressure," *Scientific American* 193, no. 5 (1955): 31–35.

or ombudsman first. The lawyer may even advise you to document your conversation if you're fearful of retaliation for asserting your right to free speech. Uncertainty tends to increase anxiety. The best plans take full advantage of points in your favor, and don't have surprise pitfalls. Knowing exactly what protections you have, as well as what protections you *don't* have, is good preparation speaking up with confidence in institutional settings.

VI. Have a "debrief date" planned with someone supportive. Even if it's just a planned phone call rather than getting together, planning a supportive conversation to occur after you speak up in a challenging situation can be helpful in three ways:

 i. It can help keep you accountable to actually *have* the "speak up conversation." You can always explain to your friend that you didn't complete the conversation if a truly good reason arises, but otherwise the planned debrief can keep you on track.

 ii. You might feel calmer and more confident during the "speak up conversation" knowing that support is on the way. Speaking up can feel risky, and having support in times of risk can mitigate stress.

 iii. If the conversation went well, your friend can help you enjoy the moment. If the conversation didn't go well, your friend is there to offer emotional support or help you strategize any next steps.

VII. Thought replacements. Thought replacements are a psychological technique where we override our predictable automatic thoughts that we have previously recognized as inaccurate or counterproductive with "replacement thoughts" that are accurate and productive. For example, an employee nervously planning to speak up in a company meeting about workplace affinity groups with views that he knows are rarely expressed (such as wondering why it's okay to have an affinity group for one demographic but not for another) predicts that from the moment he signals he'd like the floor to speak, he's likely to rattle himself with an internal monologue like, "This is stupid, what's the point of me even doing this?" These types of self-sabotaging thoughts have sandbagged him before and caused him to back down—only to kick himself later, wishing he'd had more courage. He might craft a thought replacement to silently repeat to himself like, "I'm well within my rights, I'm practicing standing up for my values, and I'm making it easier for others by breaking the ice," as a way to maintain a calm and rational mindset while he waits for the moderator to call on him.

Here's how to craft thought replacements tailored to whatever situation you wish:

   i. When you know a situation is coming where you'd like to speak up, identify if you have any predictable self-sabotaging thoughts that are likely to arise at that time. You may know them already from past experiences, or you might need to imagine yourself in the "speak up situation" to see what kinds of thoughts arise. Self-sabotaging thoughts are sometimes specific to particular people or situations. For example, you might have no problem speaking up to your friends, but you might get flooded with self-doubt when speaking up at a school board meeting.

   ii. Write down a thought that will be more productive or accurate to use in place of the old thought. The employee in the example above overrode the inaccurate thought that his actions were "stupid and pointless" with a thought that validated his behavior ("I'm within my rights") and emphasized that his actions were *not* pointless (he was practicing standing up for his values, and he was helping others).

Another example of a thought replacement to help with speaking up would be, "I won't insult others by pretending they are too weak to tolerate a difference of opinion," or, "I should give people the chance to hear my opinions before I assume they'll reject me for them," to replace automatic thoughts like, "She's so closed-minded; there's no point in even trying to talk to her." *Caveat*: There might be situations where you're correct that someone is very closed-minded. In those situations, you might judiciously decide to use healthy self-restraint, make sure you have an ally before sharing, inoculate them with a bit of information before sharing deeply, or journal privately if helpful (these techniques are discussed elsewhere in this chapter). However, if you're habitually labeling people as unworthy of inviting into dialogue because you're automatically anticipating a stone wall of rejection, it is worth considering if you might benefit from thought replacements geared toward at least giving them a chance to hear your perspective. Assuming that people are hostile to dialogue can sometimes lead us to treat them dismissively, which can be unfair if they've never even had the chance to hear our thoughts.

iii. Don't worry if your thought replacements don't feel natural at first. The whole point is that you're overriding an old way of thinking with a new way of thinking—of *course* the new way doesn't feel natural yet. Sometimes it's helpful to write down your thought replacement so you can glance at it like a script when you feel the old habitual thought arising, or make sure you have it memorized like the alphabet so it's easy to recall in moments of stress.

Helpful hint: Thought replacements are different from "positive affirmations." Positive affirmations are often aspirational, whereas thought replacements must be 100 percent accurate. If they are purely aspirational, positive affirmations have been shown to *increase* anxiety for some people, because deep down they know that they're operating from a false foundation.[2] For example, the college student above might *not* benefit from silently repeating, "I'm overflowing with confidence right now," when he *was* actually quite nervous. Do whatever feels best for you but consider carefully whether you're more likely to benefit from thought replacements that are accurate rather than aspirational.

3. Role-Play

Yes, I know role-play may sound elaborate or "over the top" if you haven't done it before, but it's actually a very common psychology technique. Role-play can be a relaxed and informative way to get comfortable sharing your thoughts and dealing with pushback or anticipated "awkward moments," or even threats of being ostracized. It lets you practice your skills and rehearse your talking points in a supportive, low-stakes environment. For example, suppose you've been on a few dates with someone, and they've made several jokes about a political figure that you admire, or they've expressed staunch views about transgenderism that differ from yours. At first, you smiled and nodded because you were just getting to know the person and didn't want to define your early interactions around political disagreements. You really like the person, and you don't mind if their sociopolitical views clash with yours—but you're nervous that they won't accept *your* views. You want to bring it up, but you're worried that your heightened anxiety about ruffling the person will, ironically, make the conversation feel awkward and tense. Role-play is a perfect way to address this. Here's how to do it, using the example above—but you can tailor the details to match whatever conversation or situation you are facing:

Step 1: Explain the situation to a friend and ask them to help you role-play by raising and completing the conversation a couple of times till it starts to feel natural.

Step 2: Consider switching roles in the conversation so that you can see how it might feel from both sides, and so that you can hear how your friend might navigate the situation you're facing.

Step 3: You might also want to ask your friend to role-play a few scenarios—perhaps one where the conversation goes well and you realize the political differences aren't a big deal, and another where the person rejects you because of the differences and you exit the budding relationship gracefully. Obviously, you prefer the former outcome, but it's good to be prepared for both outcomes, and perhaps to realize in advance that you don't truly want to be with someone who is so intolerant in the first place.

Step 4: If you "get stuck" or draw a blank in the role-play, or if you say something and realize it "doesn't sound right," don't worry—that just means that you were wise to try a role-play. Feel free to break out of the role-play for a moment and ask your friend to help you find the words—that's one of the great features of the exercise.

Role-play draws from "exposure therapy" where we deliberately experience whatever stimulus is evoking anxiety and use this experience to discover that we *can* handle the anxiety. Even if there's no anxiety-provoking stimulus, role-play can still help us to explore how certain conversations might go, "try on for size" different approaches, and brainstorm with a supportive friend about solutions to potential pitfalls. Although the example above is romantic, role-play can work well for conversations with a colleague, family member, or other life situations. Role-play is a strong stand-alone technique, or it can be a good way to test your Clear Plan for a Clear Head if you've made one.

4. The WAIT Test

This technique is designed to help make sure you are emotionally ready to speak up. Of course, there are times in life where we need to speak up whether we want to or not, but many times, it's actually up to our own discretion. As discussed in the opening to part 2, we don't want to speak up from a compulsive need to share *everything* with *everyone* and we have a right to keep certain things private. Many clients have expressed feeling so "pent up" due to censorship pressure that they reach a point where they feel tempted to overshare or share almost aggressively in a way that feels unnecessarily provocative. Other times, clients get stuck in a black-and-white approach where they have a small circle of friends who know "the real them," and everyone else gets a watered-down, sanitized "Sunday manners" version. Either way, they'd like to find a middle ground. If you're ever unsure about speaking up, or you want help expressing sensitive views in a more balanced way, the WAIT test can be a helpful way to explore the situation:

    I. <u>W</u> is for Want: Do you *want* to speak up? If you're at a dinner party and someone is making derogatory comments about people who voted the way you did, you might genuinely want to assert yourself. On the other hand, perhaps you're feeling fatigued after a long day and you'd rather just relax, and that's perfectly fine. I want you to feel empowered to speak up when you *want* to or when speaking up is a "must." Not every situation in life requires you to go out on a limb.

    II. <u>A</u> is for Appropriate: If you want to speak up, are you doing it in the appropriate time and place? For example, if you've been on a few dates with someone and you'd like to see how they'll react to learning that you have significant political differences from them, *don't* spring it on them right before the two of you arrive at a dinner party. Choose a setting that is conducive to a meaningful conversation.

III.I Is for Inoculate: You can gauge how someone is likely to respond to fulsome open dialogue, and help set the stage for deeper sharing, by first exposing them to a small slice of openness or letting them know in advance that you have something to share that might be delicate. This is helpful in situations where you want to carefully manage complex group dynamics or individual relationships but still be as open as possible. For example, you don't want to feel like you're in a verbal straitjacket with colleagues, but you also don't want to find yourself called into human resources for violating the inclusion policy due to confiding to a colleague that you find it tiresome when meeting facilitators ask you to provide your pronouns. Or you would like to be more authentic with the other parents you see regularly at your daughter's soccer games, but you want to avoid getting into a season-long snit (and possibly longer) if it turns out the group happens to be packed with people who automatically label you as "hateful" for being glad that no boys have decided to declare themselves as girls and play on the team. You'd be willing to stake a claim if a boy actually *tried* this, but otherwise it's just chatter that you'd forgo if it were going to cause a huge rift.* In these situations, it can be wise to "test the

---

* This is just an example of how *some* people might feel. It's perfectly fine if you like wearing your views on your sleeve and you don't care *who* knows how you feel. This example is about someone who has a higher threshold for sharing, but it isn't intended to be prescriptive about how much is appropriate to share in any setting.

waters" with a casual remark or question and gauge the response before sharing further ("Did you see that case about the Connecticut school girls' team where the trans players won the gold medals?").

This "water testing" exercise serves two purposes: In addition to providing a preview of what type of response a deeper expression of your views might garner, it can also set the stage for you to share without seeming as if you're "coming out of the blue." If you're sharing something that someone might find controversial, or that tends to be kept under wraps, it can be helpful to signal awareness of this so that your sharing appears measured rather than impulsive. One way to signal this is to open up gradually, rather than starting at full throttle.

IV. T is for Trust: In an environment where free speech is a fraught topic, discussing certain viewpoints can sometimes evoke feelings of being in a speakeasy, where people only feel comfortable acknowledging their true position once they know others are tolerant (not necessarily in agreement, but at least tolerant). Some of us are braver than others, but many of us feel the need to be careful about what we share and with whom. It may not be important in all cases, but if you're going to share potentially sensitive political views, the "trust factor" can come into play. For example, during the COVID-19 lockdowns, neighbors were calling hotlines to report those who dared to gather. Trust is built over frequency and duration of contact, and by building a history where respect and reliability are the norm even in the case of disagreements, along with having a mutual sense of what it means to keep certain things confidential. Share freely if you want to (in fact, I applaud those who are strong enough to share boldly). But if you feel the need to be measured, it can be helpful to pause and intentionally consider the trust factor before texting that politically incorrect meme or opening up over drinks with a colleague about what you really think of the latest diversity initiative (or what you really think about the company dropping DEI—these conversations can go both ways). Most importantly, make sure you feel you can trust *yourself* to accept whatever outcome may occur. Feeling confident in your trust level will help to facilitate openness.

Mentally checking off the steps of WAIT helps boost the chances of a successful conversation by ensuring that we're respecting our personal boundaries and sharing out of a sincere desire to connect rather than a sense of compulsion (W is for want). The WAIT system also balances the impulse to share with a sense of thoughtfulness about the most conducive time and place (A is for appropriate), and consideration of how well we know the other person (T is for trust). The exercise also includes a process to gauge the listener's reaction before we potentially overshare and make ourselves uncomfortably vulnerable with someone who isn't reacting the way we'd hoped (I is for inoculate). This can be especially important in workplace settings or other places where impression management may be essential for success in crucial aspects of our lives. The inoculation step also builds in opportunities for reciprocal disclosure, which tends to foster greater intimacy than one-way disclosure. It also aligns with Social Penetration Theory,[3] which suggests that relationships deepen through gradual increases in disclosure, moving from superficial to intimate conversations in terms of depth and breadth slowly rather than abruptly.

Vignette: Olivia Finds Her Voice

Olivia was a bright and vibrant communications associate for an ad agency in Manhattan. Just twenty-two years old, she had come to the city three years ago from a small town in North Carolina, as she had planned to do since childhood—she loved the arts and culture of New York City and had always aspired to live there. Aunt Judith was Olivia's favorite aunt. She had lived in the city's stylish West Village neighborhood since the 1990s, and she delighted in showing her niece around the city, everywhere from Broadway shows to fashion week sample sales. They had a standing Sunday brunch date, which Olivia treasured.

Olivia had long idealized her aunt and wanted to be like her in many ways, except for one: Aunt Judith was very politically liberal. This didn't bother Olivia at all; she didn't feel the need to agree with Aunt Judith on *everything*—but she was painfully aware that Aunt Judith wouldn't reciprocate her laissez-faire attitude about politics: Aunt Judith had announced on several occasions that anyone who voted for Trump was "dead to her." She would regularly deride Trump voters as bigots, rednecks, and "racist, sexist homophobes." Olivia, who actually *had* voted for Trump, initially responded by putting on a poker face and keeping the conversation moving to other topics. But inside, she became reflective. Was there something she was missing about Trump? She had certainly noticed that many, if not *all*, of the New Yorkers she met and admired seemed to share Aunt Judith's views. Was her admiration for Trump just a mark of her provinciality, and something she'd need to outgrow if she wanted to "fit in" with Aunt Judith and her West Village brunch parties? Olivia lacked the confidence to assert herself, partly because she felt so young and inexperienced compared to her sophisticated aunt.

As time passed, Olivia started to feel increasingly uncomfortable pretending to agree with her aunt about her values. In addition to differences about Trump, Olivia had seen some compelling videos online about fetal development that challenged what her aunt had always said about abortion just pertaining to "a clump of cells." These videos were often shown along with spirited online debates that put her unspoken concerns about the topic into words. As Olivia started to identify more as pro-life, she wasn't upset by Aunt Judith being staunchly pro-choice—but she was starting to feel very *fake* for nodding passively when Aunt Judith would make strong remarks with an underlying assumption that of *course* Olivia and *all* sane people agreed that "abortion rights" were part of the constitution. Olivia was approaching her mid-twenties and becoming more confident; she was starting to feel rather childish about being so afraid of her aunt's disapproval that she would hide her true opinions. At the same time, Aunt Judith had always been Olivia's "lifeline" in the city, and Olivia certainly didn't want to alienate her.

"She's actually a very intelligent and lively person, and she's been so good to me since I came to the city. It's just that when it comes to politics, she has what some people call Trump Derangement Syndrome," Olivia said with an affectionate laugh. She anticipated that a "coming out of the closet conversation" would trigger Aunt Judith to become emotional and she might even threaten to stop speaking to Olivia, and that somehow Aunt Judith would frame things as if the rift were *Olivia's* fault. Olivia's fears were reasonable: blaming and shaming "Trumpers" were tactics that her aunt had used in the past, which had made Olivia feel it was best to just hide her views and nod sheepishly at all of Aunt Judith's verbal barbs. She hadn't verbalized *agreement* with Aunt Judith, but she'd "smiled and nodded" so long that Aunt Judith probably had no idea how Olivia really felt. In fact, Olivia's *goal* had been to hide her true beliefs because she feared Aunt Judith's reaction, so Olivia knew she really couldn't even blame Aunt Judith for assuming agreement. Given this history, she feared that the "coming out conversation" could become volatile and send her into an internal spiral of thoughts like, "I should never have done this, I'm such an idiot! I'm breaking up a beautiful family relationship over political issues, what's *wrong* with me?!" Olivia disliked confrontation, so the idea of getting on Aunt Judith's "bad side" made her stomach queasy. She was afraid these thoughts would make her freeze up and back down. But she also knew the charade of agreement was wearing thin.

Olivia and I worked together to create thought replacements she could silently repeat to herself before, during, and after the conversation to help manage the thought spiral she feared. They included:

- "Close relationships are based on truth."
- "I am *not* breaking up a family relationship over politics. Aunt Judith might choose to avoid me because of *my* politics, but that is *her* choice not mine."
- "There's nothing wrong with what I'm saying, and it could actually worsen Aunt Judith's Trump Derangement Syndrome if I break down and pretend that there is."

The last thought replacement is a bit humorous, and sometimes that's helpful. If you anticipate that the conversation will become overly dramatic, a little humor can sometimes put things into perspective. Obviously, this thought replacement is certainly not one that she'd ever share with Aunt Judith. It was just to help ground Olivia in the truth that she was actually just sharing mainstream political views held by half the country, and that it would be unhelpful to *everyone*, including Aunt Judith, for Olivia to pretend as if her views truly posed an existential threat to her aunt.

Olivia prepared with role-play as well, and found that it was helpful to have go-to phrases ready, like:

- "Aunt Judith, I love you and I want us to be close. That means I have to be honest about what I believe."
- "We don't have to talk about this all day if you don't want to. I just didn't want to hide who I am. I felt you deserve to know the truth, and I deserve to be known. But now that you've heard me out— thanks for that—we could take a walk and pivot to mapping out our spring Broadway ticket plans if you'd like to change the subject."
- "I'm sorry I hid this from you. I just really love you and I was afraid of pushing you away. I understand this is probably a shock to you, but I really hope we can still be family."
- "I think if we talk more, we might realize that some of our differences are actually based on objective factual misunderstandings. I'd like to explore that with you if you want. And even if we don't ultimately agree on things, it's okay with me. I've always loved you even knowing we have our differences, and I hope you feel the same."

Olivia also used the WAIT (want, appropriate, inoculate, trust) technique to confirm she was ready for this conversation. Although she was nervous about it, she definitely *wanted* to tell her aunt the truth—hiding herself had become too uncomfortable. She chose an appropriate time and place—she didn't spring this on her aunt just as they sat down to a Broadway show; she planned a nice brunch at her apartment where they could be alone and talk things through. She also inoculated her aunt—when she texted her aunt to invite her to brunch, she mentioned there was something delicate on her mind that she was nervous to share, but that she felt it was important to discuss. As for trusting her aunt, she had to admit she didn't fully trust her aunt was going to accept her. But, she knew she could at least trust *herself* to know she had done nothing wrong, and that she was making the right choice to be authentic.

Aunt Judith *did* have difficulty with Olivia "coming out of the closet" about her true views. The initial conversation became quite charged, and Oliva was glad she had done so much practical and emotional preparation for it. The preparation helped her to remain grounded even when her aunt bristled, and to avoid escalating the emotionally laden conversation even further. Despite Olivia's best efforts, Aunt Judith was rather cool to Olivia for several months. However, she ultimately warmed as the holidays approached.

The two never reached a point of enjoying spirited discussions about their differences; instead, they "agreed to disagree" and enjoy each other's company without delving into political matters. The key difference was that Olivia no longer felt she was *hiding* herself: Aunt Judith was aware of their differences, and the two had reached an open agreement to simply leave politics on the shelf. There was no more pretending, and Olivia felt much more authentic in the new dynamic.

In the end, Olivia's experience illustrates that speaking up isn't always about changing someone else's mind—it's about reclaiming your own. Even though the outcome wasn't perfect, Olivia gained something priceless: the peace of truly being herself. She had stood firm with clarity and respect, and in doing so, gave her aunt the opportunity to know her more fully. Rather than continuing to censor herself for the sake of a false harmony, Olivia learned that true connection is built not on silent compliance, but on mutual recognition—and that sometimes, the bravest conversations lead not to agreement, but to a deeper, more honest kind of respect.

5. Narrate Your Experience

This psychological technique is deceptively simple: you just put your internal experience into words. In this case, we'll specifically focus on narrating your experience about speaking up. Done right, this can frame the conversation in a way that stimulates empathy and openness on the part of the listener. If you cue them to realize that you're feeling vulnerable or cautious about speaking up, they may respond by making an extra effort to listen respectfully as a way to reassure you that they want you to share. A few examples of how this might sound are listed below:

- (When speaking up one-to-one): "I wanted to talk with you about something that's been on my mind. I'm a little nervous about it because I don't usually put myself out there like this, but I'm trying to be more open about certain things, so I wanted to try sharing with you."
- (When speaking up at a meeting or group): "I know this perspective hasn't been raised before, but I really appreciate the encouragement we've had to contribute. So I am just going to put something out there that might sound a

little surprising but I'm hopeful maybe at least one of you
may have had a similar idea. If not, that's okay too, I just
wanted to offer the idea to the group."

- (When speaking up to a manager, professor, or other
  authority figure): "I've been hesitant to approach you
  because I don't want to seem disrespectful, but there are
  a couple of things on my mind, and I don't want to hold
  them back. Of course, I'm very open to your feedback. I
  just didn't want to be 'sitting on' these ideas, so I thought
  it might be best to raise them privately and see what you
  think."

While the technique of disclosing that you're feeling vulnerable
is likely to pave the way to greater openness on the part of the
listener,[4] remember that each situation is different and some people may not be open no matter how skillfully you frame the conversation. Consider the WAIT technique and the Seven Building
Blocks as adjuncts if you feel the need for extra support about
sharing. Also be sure to return the favor and listen carefully to
the response after you've shared. Remember: The goal isn't necessarily for them to agree with you; sometimes just knowing that
you've done your part toward fostering open dialogue by offering
your perspective and listening respectfully to others' response is
a success. Even if you don't see an immediate change or get a
categorically positive response, understand that speaking up can
still help keep lines of communication open and safeguard against
groupthink.

6. Take Ownership of Your Past Choice to Self-Censor

Make sure you're not blaming others for your past choices to
self-censor. It's true that we can feel tremendous pressure from
others to self-censor, but ultimately the decision lies within our
own control. Unless you're speaking up despite the presence of a

formal rule against what you're saying, you're likely speaking up because you've decided to stop a personal habit of self-censoring. I applaud you for that decision, and I encourage you to make it clear that you're not blaming anyone else for your past self-censorship. It's okay to acknowledge the pressures that factored into your decision to self-censor and explain you'll no longer yield to them. Recognizing your own agency in the decision has multiple benefits:

- Taking ownership of our own decisions is good for our self-efficacy, and it keeps us grounded in reality. As discussed throughout this book, speaking with clarity and accuracy is healthy on a cognitive and emotional level. Telling the truth about the fact that this was your decision bolsters your own locus of control. Psychology studies show that the more we can acknowledge what is in our own control, the better it is for our well-being.[5]
- Relationships are stronger when we can acknowledge our own mistakes rather than blaming others.[6] It will be easier for people to trust you if you're willing and able to be clear-eyed about your own role in self-censoring.
- You'll keep the lines of communication open. Just like you want to be able to speak up for yourself, it's important for others to be able to express their own opinions without worrying you'll twist that into a situation where they "silenced you" when the truth is that you chose to silence yourself.

You can use the "Narrating your Experience" technique to acknowledge your past choices and explain that you'll be more open moving forward. The exact words will differ in every situation, but here's an example of what it might look like:

"I wanted to give you a heads-up that I'm working on sharing more of myself. I've realized that sometimes I just go along with things that people say, or I don't speak up about what I think, and I'm working to change that. So, you might notice times when I share a different perspective (perhaps even right now!), and I just wanted to explain that it's about me wanting to be more authentic, and being able to 'agree to disagree' sometimes for the sake of diversity and openness."

7.   Journal and Talk to Friends, or Mind-map

If speaking up is truly impossible or ill advised, or if you just need extra practice reconnecting with your true opinions because you've stifled yourself for so long, journaling or making a point to talk openly with friends can be very helpful. As discussed in part 1, habitually stifling ourselves can eventually lead to decreased awareness of whatever material we're always stuffing down. To overcome this, make a point to "unpack" whatever parts of yourself you may feel compelled to hide in your daily life. You can do this by journaling a page at the end of the day about all the situations where you self-censored and what you would have said if you'd felt safe. You could also be intentional about discussing the material on a regular basis with someone supportive. This can be helpful to do retroactively as well. For example, I've talked to *many* psychologists who felt a great deal of pressure to conform to the "social justice agenda" during graduate school. They did such a good job of parroting the "politically correct" viewpoints they needed to succeed in classroom discussions and term papers that they almost didn't realize how much the experience was warping their true sense of themselves. In fact, this actually happened to me. Once I decided to start speaking up about how I *really* felt about certain topics, I found that I needed to journal and have supportive conversations to help "reacquaint me with my own views" and find the right words to express how I felt about certain topics. The views were there, but they were hard to articulate because I'd buried them for so long. This is why "refreshing" is often the word people use to describe how it feels to speak freely after having stifled themselves for a long time. It feels like we're *restoring* a part of ourselves that has a capacity for vibrancy but was temporarily wasting away in exile.

Vignette: Mark Reconnects with Himself

Mark was on the cusp between early career and seasoned professional. He'd been working at a hedge fund in New York for five years, and he was frustrated at not being promoted. His performance evaluations reflected a high level of skill and initiative; he arrived early and stayed late; and he worked hard to build relationships within the company. Ironically, these relationships had led a colleague in human resources to reveal to him that the company's commitment to diversity was going to present challenges to Mark's goal of earning a promotion. "There's nothing wrong with you," she had explained reassuringly. "It's just that we have a mandate to increase the diversity of our leadership—this means we need to hire people that don't look like you . . ." she trailed off.

Mark did all he could to mask his disappointment, plastering an understanding smile on his crestfallen face. "I'm sure you understand," she continued, "It's just that straight white men have run this industry for so long—"

"I totally get it," he broke in, not wanting her to regret sharing the inside track with him. In an odd way, he felt relieved. Until now, he had been second-guessing himself, wondering what more he could possibly do to obtain the promotions he was losing to colleagues whose KPI's (key performance indicators) were lower than his. At first, he had chalked up the losses to what he imagined must be a lack of "soft skills" on his part. He had worked on those, and he had tried joining the mentoring program to help junior associates, along with other ways of boosting his chances, but nothing seemed to make the critical difference needed. In a weird way, it was actually a relief to learn that his lack of promotion didn't reflect any shortcoming in terms of his skills.

After this conversation where his quiet suspicions were confirmed by his colleague from human resources, Mark put the issue aside as something beyond his control. He was restless for a while, then decided to be thankful for the well-compensated position that he *did* have in an industry he loved. He consigned himself to middle-management and redirected his extra time to sports leagues, events with his large Irish American family, and other nonprofessional activities.

As Mark relayed this story to me, he shrugged his shoulders and offered a half-hearted smile. It really didn't bother him anymore, he said. He explained that it had happened a year ago, and he had "made peace with it" by now. He only shared the story in response to my repeated questions about disappointments with women. He had offered it up with a sardonic laugh: "Well, there was the time last year when I learned I wouldn't get ahead in life because I'm a straight white dude!" Mark didn't initially connect this long-buried story to his current reason for seeking therapy, which was intimacy and commitment issues with women. He felt helpless in this regard, but he wasn't sure why.

Mark seemed surprised when I didn't laugh along with him. Instead, I repeated his story back to him, partly to ensure I had heard it correctly and partly to see how he would respond to *hearing* it said by someone who didn't feel the need to make it sound okay. Mark had gone to a lot of trouble to convince himself that this was "fine," and I was curious how he would respond to hearing the story stripped of the accommodating shoulder shrugs and affable smiles he had glossed onto it.

When Mark realized that I wasn't on the "girl power bandwagon" but was actually interested in thinking clearly about what had happened to him, I almost literally saw his guard drop. After I repeated his story and asked him if I'd heard it correctly, he dropped the half-hearted smile and shoulder-shrug routine, sat up straighter and said, "Yeah, that actually happened." When I asked if he had ever considered consulting an employment lawyer*, he paused and answered, "No, but that's an interesting idea." It was as if it had never fully occurred to him that what happened to him was *not* okay . . . but of course, it had. Mark had simply repressed his awareness to the point where he was able to shrug off this unfair treatment in the workplace.

I suggested to Mark that he begin journaling about what had happened by simply writing down the story he'd shared with me, along with any thoughts or feelings that arose for him as he pondered it. His true feelings about the situation had obviously been repressed for so long that they might need some coaxing to resurface (also Mind Mapping). He agreed and began showing up for sessions eager to share what he had written. His journaling revealed feelings of loss, as well as frustration and

---

* As a clinical psychologist, of course I don't give legal advice. However, part of my role is to encourage clients to advocate for themselves if life's circumstances or mental challenges may be obstacles to healthy self-advocacy. I felt compelled to ask Mark this question, just as I would have asked the same question to a woman who shared that she was silently tolerating sex-based discrimination because she felt powerless or undeserving of support and fair treatment.

anxiety. He also shared that he was increasingly irritated by the ongoing "diversity training" in his workplace, where he was expected to compliantly support the very principles that had led to his being overlooked for promotions he may have deserved.

I wasn't surprised that Mark's journaling preceded a burgeoning awareness that he was irritated by the diversity training. I suspected that the journaling, along with our sessions, were facilitating his willingness and ability to reconnect with a stifled part of himself: A logical part of himself that of *course* disliked programs that made it impossible for him to advance despite having the skills and work ethic to otherwise succeed. The healthy function of anxiety is to stimulate preparation behaviors, and the healthy function of anger is to stimulate boundary-setting behaviors. In this situation, the boundary that was crossed appeared to be a violation of Mark's right to fair treatment in the workplace, and he was feeling anxious because he wasn't sure what, if anything, he could do about it. Mark's newfound awareness of both anger and anxiety combined to stimulate a behavior that was helpful in terms of both preparation *and* boundary-setting. He visited an employment lawyer to explain the situation and learn about his options.

The lawyer advised Mark to revisit the conversation he'd had with the human resources colleague and see if he could get her to reiterate her previous acknowledgment that "straight white males' were at a disadvantage for leadership promotions, and to record it (laws about recording conversations are different in every state, but in New York this is legal). Once he had the recording, his lawyer said they would be able to approach Mark's employer to discuss the situation and likely end with a settlement and a nondisclosure agreement. Mark took some time to ponder this but said that it felt validating and vindicating to know he had legal options he could exercise regardless of whether he pursued them.

Mark did ultimately decide to pursue the situation, and it turned out to be a "win" more than just legally—confronting the situation of being passed over partly because he was a man led him to explore an assumption he'd made about women, which was ultimately helpful in his initial goal of getting past his resistance to intimacy and commitment. Partly because Mark's initial reason for seeking therapy was his difficulty with intimacy and commitment with women, I had asked Mark how the women in his workplace reacted to the diversity training sessions, especially those that dealt with the need to promote women in the workplace. He responded, "They love them, of course—all women do, right?" As we talked more, he acknowledged that it was possible that at least *some* women were uncomfortable with the idea of their sex being a factor in workplace promotions, yet (just like him) they may have felt it would be unwise to express this openly. As Mark learned to assert his objections to these diversity programs, and as he went through a multimonth period of dealing with the legal case, he naturally became more expressive about the topic in his personal life. As he dated with this newfound expressiveness, he came to see that many women actually viewed his situation sympathetically. Because he was no longer pretending to himself that what had happened at work was "fine," he became more authentic in his personal life, too. This naturally paved the way to greater openness and feeling genuinely accepted by the women he dated, which helped greatly with his capacity for intimacy and commitment.

He was living life with his *whole self* instead of stifling parts that he imagined would be "politically incorrect," and this made all the difference in finding the deeper relationships he craved.

Chapter 6

Five Tools for Self-Restraint

I believe in the power of listening to one another, even when we disagree, because it's the only way we can find common ground.
—BARACK OBAMA

While the majority of this book has emphasized the importance of speaking up and tools to do so, we must remember that listening is an essential part of open dialogue. In many ways, it's just as important as speaking. In my early days of training as a psychologist, I often felt compelled to jump in and offer solutions or insights to justify the time or expense that clients were investing into therapy. While it's important for a therapist to offer helpful input, even the wisest words will fall on deaf ears if they're spoken too soon. "Listening is doing, Chloe," one of my favorite supervisors used to tell me to calm my overeager style. He wanted me to know that listening exquisitely—really taking the time to understand the client on a deep level by listening carefully and without judgment—was a foundational step to building deep rapport and trust and ultimately laying the groundwork for growth. Even if your goal isn't ultimately to help the person grow, listening well can enrich your dialogue tremendously. In this chapter, we'll unpack the primary benefits of listening and provide a set of tools to help you listen resiliently.

Listening seems so simple: All you have to do is sit there and say nothing, right? It's easy! Fact check: false. As anyone who has ever sat listening to someone who is saying things that are offensive, inaccurate, or misguided about a topic close to your heart, sometimes "just listen" is much easier said than done. However, listening well is crucial to meaningful dialogue. It reduces defensiveness on the part of the speaker, gives you (as the listener) an opportunity to challenge any assumptions you might have about the speaker's positions and helps to build or strengthen rapport. Being a good listener can also help the speaker to become reflective about what they're saying, as discussed in the Gifts of Language chapter.

Another benefit of listening well—one that's a bit sneaky, actually—is that it can lead people to reciprocate and give you a chance to share your views, and potentially even make them more persuadable. Research shows that when a person perceives someone is listening carefully to them, it activates a positive mental state. That positivity causes the person to evaluate the listener more positively on an emotional level, thereby making them more cooperative with that person and potentially more open to their perspective. In fact, research participants who were listened to carefully showed activation in the ventral striatum, which is a key part of the brain's "reward system" —the same system that is activated when we win at gambling or enjoy a cocktail. In other words, good listeners are like a drug that produces a pleasant high—it feels good to us, and we'll "lean in" to people who provide it. I want you to listen well because it's good for open dialogue—but if you need extra motivation to hold your tongue when things get heated, just remember that listening might actually help you win an argument or two.

What does it mean to "listen well"? For starters, it means not interrupting. It also means doing more than just keeping quiet while waiting for your turn to talk. It means giving your best effort to understand what the person is saying, rather than jumping to conclusions about why they hold particular positions. It means asking questions and being willing to understand a new perspective, or even potentially to revise your own. Last but not least, it means making space for the possibility that reasonable people can disagree. Even if you and the other person will never see eye to eye, you can still respect one another and have a good relationship despite your disagreements. In fact, sometimes relationships are enhanced by a diversity of perspectives. Supreme Court justices Antonin Scalia and Ruth Bader Ginsberg were a paragon of building a good relationship despite differences. Although they were essentially polar political opposites, they had a standing weekly lunch date, vacationed together with their families, and shared a deep mutual respect, both personally and professionally. "We were best buddies," said Justice Bader Ginsberg of Justice Scalia. If these Supreme Court justices with such stark differences could work together on matters of public policy and build a friendship for the history books, surely the rest of us can at least try to listen a little better to friends, family, coworkers, or others in our lives who see things differently.

Caveat: The goal is not to listen to abusive language. If someone is calling you names, swearing at you, or otherwise belittling you, then listening is likely no longer productive. Respecting the free speech rights of others and seeking to have open dialogue doesn't mean we have to relinquish basic personal boundaries and standards. You're always free to assert your boundaries or even end the conversation altogether if it's no longer productive. Depending on the situation, you might want to do this gently with an invitation to continue the conversation when the person can be more respectful, or with the intention of moving on more permanently. You might even decide to review the conversation with a lawyer, an ombudsman, or your human resources department. You don't have to tolerate abuse, and the techniques for listening should not be taken to suggest otherwise. However, in many situations, you may find that listening openly and patiently will pave the way for rich, meaningful dialogue that deepens your relationships and facilitates a two-way street of authenticity, while also enriching your own perspective and body of knowledge.

As a psychologist, I have spent thousands of hours listening to clients with a wide variety of viewpoints. Sometimes it's easy, and sometimes it's hard. For times when it's hard, here are some practical tools that I encountered or developed along the way. I hope they are helpful. As always, please feel free to share with me through my website or on social media and let me know how the tools work for you, or if you have any variations as well as any "stumpers." I love hearing from readers!

1. "Find the Facts"

This technique helps when you're feeling tempted to interrupt, or you have an awareness that you're being overly confrontational. If you're struggling to hold your tongue and be a respectful listener, it can be helpful to give your brain a productive "side task" to help divert the part of you that is dying to interrupt while also keeping you focused on what the other person is saying. A side task of mentally "checking out" to review your weekend plans while you pretend to listen, or a side task of mentally preparing how your response would *not* count as productive.

    I.   The first productive side task is to listen carefully for a fact, or the implication of a fact, that you didn't know. Be genuinely open-minded to the possibility that you may have something to *learn*. Many Americans, for example, genuinely believe that Donald Trump was referring to neo-Nazis when he said there were "fine people on both sides" in Charlottesville, despite him actually saying the opposite.[1] If this many Americans could be misinformed about something so important, perhaps there's something *you* need to learn as well. Recognize that learning something new is a badge of honor, not "getting owned," as many social media video titles might suggest. Done well, this step can stimulate you to ask genuine questions of the other person, rather than just cutting them off to make your own point. If you do learn something new, be sure to acknowledge it. This can be a great bridge-builder in conversation. *Caveat:* While it's good to learn from others, it's also helpful to verify factual information as much as possible. If you learn something surprising during the course of conversation, look it up to confirm. Similarly, if someone doubts your facts, be open to looking them up as well. You can use your own judgment depending on the nature of the conversation to decide if real-time lookups or post-conversation lookups will be most productive (in some situations, it might seem confrontational, whereas in others it might be received as an earnest openness to learning). Also, be wary of confirmation bias; if you have a preconceived idea about a topic, you're less likely to notice or agree with information that challenges it.[2] Even if it's just to keep yourself sharp, take the challenge seriously to see if you can spot a new fact. This will also be a good rapport builder since people will sense that your mind is genuinely open to learning something new.

II. If you truly can't discover a fact that you didn't know, don't give up on listening. The second side task is to try and spot any objectively *factual* errors in the person's narrative. When you find one, *don't pounce on it.* Instead, take a slow deep breath and remember your goals for the conversation (perhaps to reduce stress by improving family relationships). Try the "Relax Your Body—and Your Mouth!" technique (Tool Two in this chapter). Think about something you really like or respect about the person, if possible. If you can't find anything, it might be a sign that you're in too much of a black-and-white mindset to mention the errant fact you've spotted in a truly non-confrontational way. In most cases, we can at least admire that someone is a good family man, an intelligent person, a charismatic communicator, or *something*.

Once you've taken a deep breath, relaxed your body, located something likeable about the person, and have been listening long enough to believe this person can't share any new facts with you but perhaps you've located an error in their narrative, you've probably been listening long enough to jump in and ask if they'd like to hear your thoughts. If they say yes, you could even mention the factual error you may have spotted but be sure to do so in a friendly way and volunteer the source of your information. Be willing to listen more if they respond that they just want to finish their thought. Try not to get frustrated, because their response that they'd like to communicate the rest of their point may actually mean that you're doing a *great* job at listening and bridge-building. If you find the person is going "on and on," consider inviting them to do the Reflective Listening technique.

2. Relax Your Body—and Your Mouth!

When others are saying things that you find offensive or that are factually incorrect about something important to you, it's hard to keep quiet and listen, and it's easy to get caught in a fight-or-flight reaction even where there's no physical danger. During these times, we may be prone to physical tension and verbal outbursts such as barbs, frequent interruptions, or even just a testy vocal tone. It's like we're "champing at the bit" to make our point. This not only fails to *help* the conversation, but it often *hurts* the conversation by turning people off or sending signs of escalation. World-renowned couples therapist John Gottman's research[3] suggests that when our heart rate rises above 100 beats per minute, it becomes nearly impossible to listen and communicate effectively. He recommends taking a twenty-minute break at times like that—which is helpful, but not always practical. Here's another way you can manage your physical fight-or-flight reaction and its verbal manifestations (such as a clenched jaw, pursed lips, or an overactive mouth that seems constantly poised to interrupt) to be a good listener, and help keep the conversation peaceful and productive—while also keeping your mind clear and nimble:

I. When you notice yourself getting riled during a conversation to the point where you become testy or interrupt, the first thing to do is to congratulate yourself on your awareness. It takes a lot of courage and self-awareness to recognize and admit when you're getting triggered, and it will be easier to keep up the good work of recognizing this if you respond positively to your awareness rather than by castigating yourself or feeling ashamed. Many people become obstinate about charged topics, but it takes a very mature person to realize it. So please, start by congratulating yourself.

II. Take a slow deep breath and remember your goals for the conversation (perhaps to reduce stress by improving family relationships, or to learn more about why and how someone might see an issue differently than you do).

III. Relax your throat, your lips, your tongue, and your jaw. It's natural to hold tension in these areas when we're feeling tempted to engage in a verbal argument. The physical muscles of speech can start activating and becoming tense, even if the tension is part of your efforts to "hold your tongue." Your lips can become pursed, your jaw clenched, and even your tongue or throat can feel tight. When the "caveman" part of our brain has a fight-or-flight reaction and is unconsciously preparing for physical confrontation, our shoulder blades and hands can become clenched as well. But by relaxing the body, we can cue the mind to relax as well. One way to do this is to take a breath in and then imagine those areas relaxing as you exhale. Some people find it helpful to visualize their exhalation going into the physical area they'd like to relax. You can do one exhalation at a time for each part you'd like to relax, or just focus on general relaxation as you exhale. Exhaling is part of the parasympathetic nervous system, whereas inhaling pertains to the sympathetic nervous system. The parasympathetic nervous system is the part that helps us calm down, which is why this step centers around exhalation.

Think about something you really like or respect about the person, if possible. In most cases, we can at least admire that someone is a good family man, an intelligent person, a charismatic communicator, or *something*. You may notice this step and the beginning of the next step dovetail with the steps of the Find the Facts technique. This is because taking a deep breath and mentally reviewing what you like about the speaker can be useful in a variety of situations when you're experiencing frustration but want to project a calm demeanor and avoid lapsing into black-and-white thinking, where you might be prone to paint everything about the person as negative due to one or two disagreeable points they are making.

    IV. Once you've taken a deep breath, relaxed your body, and located something likeable about the person, hopefully you are now poised to speak up in a way that will enrich the dialogue. If not, it's okay to say, "I am sorry,* but I find myself feeling really charged right now on this topic. Would it be okay if we pick this up later? Can we pivot to ___?" Suggesting a new topic is helpful because it conveys that you feel the need to exit the conversation, but not to reject the *person*. It will also make it cognitively easier for the other person to switch gears if you mention something new for their brain to latch onto. Otherwise, just telling the person to drop whatever they've been discussing is like saying, "Don't think about pink elephants." It ironically reinforces the topic you're trying to minimize. Good pivot topics include weekend plans, noncontroversial current events, or any other item you have in common with the person. Saying you want to exit the current topic but inviting the person onto another topic will feel much smoother than just making a halting statement that the conversation is over.

Vignette: Andrew Learns to Listen

Andrew was a talented technology specialist in his mid-thirties who was struggling with depression and living an increasingly isolated life because he felt perpetually victimized by exposure to colleagues or family members who expressed positive regard for things he felt

---

* For those who are concerned about apologizing when they've done nothing wrong: Don't worry, you're not apologizing for having done something "wrong" here. This is the same sort of apology we give when we're invited somewhere but need to decline—we simply say, "I'm sorry, I can't make it." It doesn't imply we've done anything wrong. In this case, you're saying you're sorry because you've been "invited" to a topic of conversation and you're not feeling up to pursuing it. Rest assured, this form of apology is just a social convention to acknowledge that you're the one who is stopping things from moving forward on this topic, not an indication that you've done anything wrong.

were hateful (i.e., celebrating Supreme Court ruling that effectively ended affirmative action). He labeled these people as "bullies" and refused to discuss or debate the issues with them, because he felt their viewpoints were hateful (he often described these viewpoints as transphobic, homophobic, xenophobic, misogynistic, etc.) Andrew sought therapy to cope with the perceived "trauma" of exposure to these hateful people and to prepare himself for "going no contact"* with his sister, who volunteered at a pro-life clinic and strove to live a "color-blind" life. Andrew generally liked his sister—she was sweet, funny, and frequently called or texted to see how he was doing or to invite him for a meal—but he found her attitudes on abortion and race to be provincial and hateful, so this meant she had to be banished from his "hate-free life."

Andrew had a small group of friends whom he saw regularly, and they considered themselves to be "social justice warriors." Unfortunately, he struggled to be totally open with them. Their conversations often centered around social or political oppression, which generally implied there was a marginalized victim and a counterpart aggressor, and the aggressor was typically labeled as "hateful," a "bully," a "fascist," or a "Nazi." Andrew was, understandably, afraid that if he were too open with them he might somehow accidentally say something that could land him in the "aggressor" category, which would mean that he would

---

* "Going no contact" is a term that is (sadly) gaining in popularity. The term refers to cutting off contact completely and permanently with family members or other formerly integral people in one's life, often over ideological differences.

Joshua Coleman and Will Johnson, "How Estrangement Has Become an Epidemic in America," *Time*, December 13, 2024, https://time.com/7201531/family-estrangement-us-politics-epidemic-essay/.

likely be ejected from the friend group. As a heterosexual white male, Andrew was painfully aware that his "white privilege," "male privilege," "cis privilege," and "straight privilege" made him dangerously close to membership in the "systems of historic oppression" that operated the alleged levers of hatred his group opposed so strongly. In other words, Andrew didn't feel secure in his relationships. He didn't live in social circles where people worked out their differences amicably, and sometimes "agreed to disagree." His world was more "live by the social justice sword, die by the social justice sword." This felt like a harsh way to navigate life, Andrew admitted, but he saw it as his responsibility to "do the work" and face life's tough realities.

I debated how to respond to Andrew's request for support in preparing himself for "going no contact" with his sister. Social support is essential to mental well-being, and Andrew's sister seemed (by Andrew's own description) to be one of the most secure relationships in his life. Although she disagreed with him just as much as he disagreed with her on sociopolitical issues, Andrew felt she would be very unlikely to ever initiate limiting contact with him. I was concerned about facilitating Andrew's isolation of himself into a crowd where he admitted the social bonds were tenuous. I also didn't want to collude with, or inadvertently validate, the idea that pulling his sister out of his life like a toxic weed seemed sensible and healthy. On the other hand, since Andrew had made it clear that his goal was to "eradicate hate" from his life by removing anyone who disagreed with him on what he called social justice issues, I was concerned that challenging him might destroy our rapport along with any chance of an intervention to help him build deeper relationships that could withstand political disagreement.

After careful consideration, I gave Andrew psychoeducation about the importance of stable relationships that can withstand a diversity of opinions, and I encouraged him to consider exploring a few investigatory steps before "going no contact" since his sister appeared to be one of the most stable and accepting relationships in his life. I told him he was obviously free to end contact with her at any time, but that his satisfaction with that decision would probably be higher in the long term if he could look back knowing that he tried every reasonable step prior to ending contact. After learning more about what those steps might be, Andrew agreed to give them a try.

Here is an overview the techniques he used and why they worked:

a. Thought Replacements: Andrew developed thought replacements to use when exposed to sociopolitical ideas he disliked. Andrew had developed what psychologists call "automatic thoughts" in response to hearing people express certain sentiments his sister happened to espouse, such as her belief in term limits on abortion and her feeling of relief that her son (a white male) would be able to compete for college admissions on an equal playing field in terms of SAT scores, GPA, and other factors that have been demonstrated to disadvantage white or Asian students when race-based affirmative action is used in college admissions.[4] Andrew's automatic internal response to these sentiments was to think, "You racist, fascist bitch!" I know, it sounds extreme, but this is what Andrew admitted was his internal response when I asked him to describe the internal monologue that arose when his sister shared about these topics. After careful thought and consideration, Andrew agreed to temporarily override his automatic thought with a silent mantra, "You may be misguided, but you're my sister and perhaps you'll see the light like I did."

b. Relax Your Body—and Your Mouth!: Andrew found this technique paired well with his efforts at overriding confrontational thoughts with more amicable thought replacements. By intentionally inviting relaxation into his body, he found it was much easier to keep his thoughts peaceful and remain open-minded.

c. Reflective Listening. Andrew invited his sister to try this technique from couples therapy where each person shares their views and repeats back what the other person said, to ensure a deeper level of understanding (this technique is described step-by-step in the previous chapter). One key takeaway Andrew found from this exercise was that his sister did agree that racism was reprehensible and certainly had no place in college admissions or professional hiring decisions; she simply disagreed on what would be the most effective strategy to remove racism and sexism from those processes. Andrew had heard his sister say this before, but he had glossed over it in his rush to make his own counterpoint, or in his distraction by his historic automatic thoughts about her being a "racist, fascist bitch." The Reflective Listening exercise helped him to slow down and *reflect* on what she was saying more deeply than he'd previously done. He had to admit that at least her heart was in the right place.

d. Find the Facts: Since Andrew prided himself on his intellect, he was happy to agree to this exercise.

It also gave his brain a welcome diversion when he felt tempted to go down the old "racist, fascist bitch" thought path that he'd agreed to avoid temporarily. As he listened to his sister, he found they did agree on the fact that there was absolutely nothing genetic about any racial group that should disqualify or disadvantage them from holding any job or attending any school. He initially disagreed with her when she asserted that Asian students must perform approximately 400 points better on the SAT than black students with similar academic credentials in order to be admitted to Ivy League schools,[5] but was surprised when she sent him a requested reference. It wasn't exactly a factual disagreement, but he did find it interesting to drill down and discover that his sister was actually very open to colleges using income-based programs to help economically disadvantaged students in admissions, and she acknowledged that this would likely have a disproportionate impact on black students due to economic disparities—her concern with including a purely racial factor was partly that it could advantage wealthy black students over very poor white students, for example. Andrew was surprised that his sister's viewpoint might actually have a "social justice" component to it after all.

Andrew found his conversations with his sister to be stimulating in multiple ways: there were intellectual points that intrigued him, and they caused him to consider that rigidly silencing others could also be seen as "hateful," which was exactly the opposite of the self-concept he wanted to cultivate. He was also able to bolster his sense of self-efficacy and self-esteem by realizing he was strong enough to set boundaries and remain grounded in his values despite exposure to disagreement. Given the relationship between helplessness and depression, this was an important step. Perhaps most importantly, he was able to stop a painful isolation that would further weaken his social support system and likely increase his vulnerability to depression.

3.   Imagine an Audience.

Have you ever noticed that you're on your "best behavior" when others are watching? You're not alone. Research shows (Bateson, Nettle, and Roberts 2006)[6] that a sense of being watched can spark reputational concerns and enhanced cooperation. This is why if you're struggling to maintain your composure in a charged conversation and you're tempted to start making barbs or frequent interruptions, it can be helpful to imagine that your conversation is being viewed by someone whose opinion of you matters. It could be a person you admire for their interpersonal skills, your mentor, or just someone you'd like to impress. For some people, it's their mother. For others, it's their spouse or their children. For religious people, it could be God. You don't even have to actually know the person; if there's a particular historical figure that you admire, that could work well too. I've even had anger management clients tell me they imagined *I* was watching when they felt tempted to go offtrack. You might even imagine the interaction is being taped and will soon go viral online, and you want to make sure the video reflects well on you. The goal is just to activate your sense of social accountability along with your goals of how you'd like to be perceived by others.

Bonus: This technique would likely work for speaking up as well, if you feel yourself getting unnecessarily snippy or heated.

4. Count the Minutes, Count the Questions, and Transfer the Grace

This technique works best when you need or want to build rapport with someone who is expressing sociopolitical beliefs that seem unfounded to the point where the beliefs feel delusional, especially if the person becomes angry and unwilling to listen when presented with facts that challenge their narrative.[7] Of course, there's no rule that says you *have* to build rapport with such a person; there's nothing wrong with simply keeping your distance or dropping the relationship if the person is truly insufferable. However, in some situations we may feel it's worth "hanging on" for the sake of the relationship. Far too many families have been severed over theoretical, academic, and sociopolitical disagreements. Particularly when dealing with people who are very young (age twenty-five and under), it can be wise to mentally extend grace and remember that many of us held beliefs in college or graduate school that now seem naive, wacky, or worse.

Building rapport with a loved one is a worthy goal in itself, but an additional benefit of building rapport is that it may create an opening for the person to eventually become more receptive to hearing *your* perspective as well. If you do this technique long enough, oftentimes the speaker will eventually start to feel awkward doing *all* the talking, and they'll nudge you to respond. If not, at least you've engaged the person and modeled what it looks like for a mature person to *really* listen respectfully despite having stark differences in perspective.

The technique is simple:

I. See how many minutes you can go without speaking, except to ask sincere questions. Count the number of minutes you can remain silent and count the number of questions you can ask during your listening session.

II. If you struggle to keep quiet because the prattle feels so foolish, mentally recall times in your life when *you* were a bit (or very) jejune about a topic or a movement—perhaps even a teenage "fashion phase" you once celebrated that now makes you cringe. Mentally give yourself grace for those cringe-worthy times when you were young, inexperienced, and well-meaning but misguided, and then extend that same grace to the person speaking now. There are exceptions, of course. If the speaker starts calling you names or outright insulting you, it makes sense to end the conversation. But otherwise, challenge yourself to see how long you can listen, how many questions you can ask, and how much grace you can transfer.

III. Don't worry that listening and asking thoughtful questions will imply that you agree with the person. It's understandable that you wouldn't want to be misperceived as validating what may be very dysfunctional ideas. If you feel the need to clarify that generous listening and thoughtful questions do *not* imply your agreement or validation, you can phrase your questions carefully to put a very fine point on the fact that you're simply trying to *understand*. Questions like, "From your perspective, what is the . . ." or "When did you first start to see things this way?" can be helpful.

As a clinical psychologist, I've found this approach helps me to explore a client's perspective deeply, and ultimately to be more effective in my goals of building rapport so that I can introduce new ideas—even if the client's perspective is outright delusional. In fact, the more maladaptive a client's thought process is, the more important it can be to make *sure* I fully understand it and that I have built rapport (even if it's painfully difficult to follow their nonsensical delusions) before I attempt any interventions.

I learned this in my very early days of training. I was working with a schizophrenic patient who suffered from delusions of persecution; he believed his phone was tapped by German spies who communicated with him through the radio. My supervisor gave me a great tip: She told me not to make the rookie mistake of trying to "hit this client over the head" by immediately giving him exercises that challenged the delusions. Instead, she suggested that I ask questions about what the spies told him, if they tended to communicate more during certain times of day, and if the client ever responded to the spies (and if yes, what he said). She explained to me that although the client was living in a fantasy world, my first job was to *understand* the world and what it represented to him. Once I understood the client's inner world more fully, I would be better equipped to see what next steps to take. Would it eventually make sense to challenge the delusions? Or merely use my leverage of rapport to at least find ways to help the client limit his engagement with the delusions? Or wait patiently for the client to eventually express some doubt about the delusions, and *then* explore the doubt? Or some other strategy altogether? Before I could answer these questions, I would need to *understand* the client and gain his trust.

Although you're not a clinical psychologist working with delusional patients, you might be a loving relative who is encountering a family member suffering a delusion that she is living under great oppression. The same principles that helped me with my schizophrenic patient can actually be helpful in everyday life as well, such as wanting to keep a loved one close even if they seem consumed with delusional beliefs. If your goal is to preserve the relationship and potentially help them to see a different perspective, good listening skills may help you to build closeness that you can eventually leverage in order to help them revise their outlook whenever the timing is right.

5. Thought Replacements

This technique was discussed in the "Tools for Speaking Up" chapter already, so I won't review the entire set of directions about it here. But it appears in the "Tools for Self-Restraint" chapter as well because this technique can actually work for *both* situations—it just depends on whether the thought replacements are geared towards speaking up, or toward self-restraint. Every situation will be different, but here are a few potential thought replacements:

I. "Listening doesn't mean agreeing." This is helpful for people who struggle to listen because they feel an almost compulsive desire to interject and ensure their quiet, gentle listening doesn't signify they accept what the other person is saying. They don't want to be seen as "smiling and nodding" when they actually disagree completely. This concern can become especially active when discussing charged topics that touch our sense of morality. One healthy function of anger is to stimulate boundary-setting behaviors, so when a person is saying things that make us feel charged, we may need to reassure ourselves that simply listening and allowing their words into our mind will *not* in itself "break our boundaries." It's easy to grasp the point that "listening doesn't mean agreeing" when we're in a calm state, but it can be a helpful "lifeboat" to silently repeat when we're feeling heated and might otherwise lose sight of this simple truth. As a reminder, you *always* have the right to end a conversation, especially if the person becomes disrespectful. This technique is to help you listen despite strong disagreement, not to tolerate being mistreated.

II. "I am building my listening skills." This deceptively simple thought replacement has several layers: it reminds you that your goal is to listen, activates your sense of pride in being a good listener, and underscores that listening is a *skill*. Reminding yourself that regardless of what the person is saying, you are actively practicing an important skill can help to depersonalize the interaction and give you a tiny bit of emotional distance. That distance can act as a salve on whatever irritation or boredom may be arising from the other person's input.

III. Silently repeat what they say. This is similar to reflective listening because it involves repeating what the other person has said, but it's actually a very different exercise because you don't necessarily repeat aloud, there's no structured time limit on how long you might listen, and you're not expecting the other person to eventually reflect your thoughts back to you. You're not doing one-sided reflective listening as a way of "backing your way" into the partner technique as described for a variation of this technique in the previous chapter. Your focus is exclusively on listening, and you are simply, silently repeating their basic points or keywords to stay focused while you listen (you don't need to repeat verbatim; that could quickly become unwieldy). This is not technically a thought replacement since it doesn't involve a pre-scripted line that you mentally repeat to yourself, but it's included here because it's a predetermined plan where a script is provided for you to mentally repeat. The script is just whatever the other person is saying. This helps keep you attend to what they're saying, and prevents you from spiraling into your own reactions, including mentally preparing your response to the point where you're no longer listening. Your mental goal of silently repeating the key words facilitates a deeper level of cognitive processing because you have to actively evaluate the content of what they're saying to determine which words are central to their narrative. People can tell when you're really listening, and it tends to help conversations.[8] As the colloquialism goes, they want to "feel heard."

While this is different from the partner-based version of Reflective Listening described earlier, you can still recap what the speaker said when it feels like the appropriate time to respond in the conversation ("So if I hear you correctly, your perspective is that . . ."). It can be incredibly disarming when the speaker realizes that you're a generous listener who is focusing deeply on simply hearing them; and that even when you "have the floor" you are only using it to focus on your understanding of what they said.

You may wonder when to use this version of Reflective Listening versus the full version. This variation is best when you want to be intentional about just listening without trying to insert your own viewpoint. It can also be an excellent way to keep rapport by being a good listener and tracking the speakers' points attentively even when they are long-winded or sharing material that you find difficult to digest because it is complex or disagreeable. This next part is a bit controversial, but this variation can also be a good technique to help someone realize the flaws in their thinking without making a direct challenge to their thought process. Sometimes, hearing our views reflected back in a neutral, nonjudgmental manner can stimulate reflection and metacognition; repeating someone's thoughts back to them gives them a unique opportunity to review what they have said. Being passive-aggressive isn't always maladaptive: As discussed in chapter 3, passive aggression can actually be adaptive in certain circumstances, especially when we're using it consciously and intentionally.

It's actually an extremely common technique for therapists to use one-sided reflective listening in therapy sessions. If a client is describing a maladaptive perspective and seems likely to have a defensive reaction if the therapist makes a direct challenge, the therapist can simply repeat it back as a way to affirm to the client that they're listening carefully, while also subtly cuing the client to "hear themselves" and potentially reflect upon their words. However, this technique will fail miserably if the speaker hears any needling judgment or biting incredulity in your voice as you reflect their words back to them. You must strive to present as if your main goal is to affirm that you have heard and understood them correctly. (Hopefully, that really is your main goal— but realistically, it's understandable that there may be times when you also have a strong hope that the speaker might ultimately have a change of perspective, or you may even have a sense of revulsion about their current views.) If you need help finding an empathetic tone as you reflect their words back to them, try to consider the speaker's life experiences that may have led to their views. Try the "Relax Your Body—and Your Mouth" technique, or just keep listening quietly and silently repeating their key words as a way to maintain focus. Listening attentively is an amazing tool to build empathy and rapport.

IV. Ask yourself, "What does this person need from me right now?" or "What emotion is this person feeling right now?" These questions activate your empathy, and they can provide a bridge-building detour away from feelings of excessive intensity that arise when we feel overly pulled to "win" an argument. The first question also increases our sense of control, as it highlights our agency within the conversation—and a sense of control helps us to remain calm. The second question is likely to boost emotional attunement with the speaker, which can be helpful if the conversation is getting heated (research has shown a boost in mirror neuron activity, discussed in the Emotional Gifts of Language chapter, when actively trying to process facial emotions).

Sometimes, the answer to the first question might be that the person needs us to acknowledge that we understand at least *some aspect* of a point they've made, even if we don't agree with it ("So you're saying that increasing levels of legal gun ownership could actually reduce violence. I see it differently, but it seems we at least share the same goal."). Other times, the person might just need to be heard, or for us to say something that indicates we like them or respect them, or to acknowledge we've learned *something* from what they've said, no matter how minor it may seem. ("Well, thanks for sharing with me about that. You're an intelligent person, and I can see you've thought a lot about this. I didn't know that cities with the strictest gun control laws actually have the highest rates of gun violence, that's an intriguing fact. I might not respond to it the same as you do, but thanks for highlighting it. It's an interesting point.")

Silently asking these two simple questions can help avoid the pitfalls of a brain that is hyper-focused on a particular point or getting drawn into conflict. They help us "zoom out" and reconnect with the human side of an interaction.

Vignette: Bill and Sarah Play the Long Game

Bill had always enjoyed a good relationship with his daughter, Sarah. That is, until recently when she went to a New England college and became a gender studies major. Since then, she had dyed her hair blue and constantly made derogatory remarks about "the patriarchy," white people, heterosexual people, and what she called the "systemic oppression and misogyny inherent to the United States." Bill was an army veteran, and he took her remarks personally—he had fought long and hard alongside his fellow soldiers to protect the freedoms of *all* people in the United States. His wife told him to simply avoid the topic of politics with Sarah, but Bill didn't want to do that. He didn't want to "run away" from their disagreements; he said it would feel like they were just "pretending" instead of dealing with the fact that some significant differences had developed between them. Moreover, he was genuinely concerned that Sarah was internalizing a warped sense of reality. His first instinct was to debate Sarah; he believed it was the best way to help her see some serious flaws in her logic. However, the more he tried to engage with her in a fact-based, logical manner, the more rigidly she adhered to her own talking points. And the more Sarah did this, the more strident Bill became about *his* talking points. Bill and Sarah were stuck in what psychologists call "group polarization." Group polarization is when people on opposite sides of an argument get *farther* apart because each side senses that the other is unwilling to acknowledge the validity of the opposing side, so they both become more deeply entrenched in "defending their territory" and therefore less open to viewing the matter flexibly. Even if you're right, you won't "win" an argument in this situation.

Bill eventually realized that these debates were failing on all fronts: He was not convincing Sarah of anything, and worse, his relationship with her was suffering greatly. He decided to try something different. Next time Sarah made a derogatory remark about "the patriarchy," Bill simply asked a question—not a pointed question intended to expose an error in her logic, but a question simply intended to draw her out. He would ask her to share about her personal experiences with this issue, when and how she began learning about it, and what professors or authors she admired most in these areas of study. He would even ask her to share about the term papers she had written and what the classroom discussions about these topics were like. Sarah would often give long-winded answers that used to bother Bill because he found them pompous, and of course her verbosity made it difficult to "break in" with his own point. But shifting his focus to simply counting how many minutes he could listen, and how many *good* questions he could ask, made listening easier. He even learned a few interesting facts, some of which he was able to verify by looking them up later, and some of them he discovered seemed to be dubious—but he held his tongue on challenging Sarah since he had decided to focus exclusively on listening for a while.

At first, he was surprised by how few minutes (or even seconds) elapsed before he found himself checking his watch to see how long he'd been listening. Eventually, he built his listening time up to ten, fifteen, and even twenty minutes. When Bill found himself feeling triggered by what he viewed as Sarah's arrogant attitude or profound ignorance, he silently recalled how he used to mentally vilify his superiors in the army. He'd been a very young man when he enlisted (about Sarah's age, actually), and he had imagined his commanding officers were simply "overbearing assholes." It wasn't until years later that he realized that his commanding officers were actually admirable, hardworking men and women who took their sacred commitment to training soldiers *very* seriously; and that they went to great pains to enforce high standards for everyone's *safety*. Remembering his own folly gave Bill the perspective he needed in order to extend some grace to Sarah, and to just keep *listening* to her. He also tried the "Relax Your Body, Relax Your Mouth" technique when she said things that were particularly vexing. This went on for several months.

Eventually, Sarah shared that she was upset because a professor had told her to "check her white privilege" at a time when Sarah was actually quite certain that her so-called white privilege had nothing to do with the situation. This moment offered a thread that Bill could subtly pull upon. It was a crack in Sarah's foundation of trust that her professors were paragons of social justice. Bill knew Sarah never would have confided in him about this if he had constantly undermined her views; she wouldn't have wanted to give him the "ammunition" with which to assail her position. But because he had remained a trustworthy sounding board, he was able to stay close enough to become a resource when Sarah's nonsensical beliefs bumped up against a challenge that *she* was ready to see in a more clear-eyed manner. When this happened, Bill invited Sarah to try the Reflective Listening technique. Because he had worked so diligently to understand her perspective and to build rapport, and because he had patiently waited till there was at least a tiny opening in her mind to hearing diverse perspectives, the exercise went well. Sarah didn't do an intellectual turnabout where she abandoned her own ideas and came into full agreement with Bill, but at least Bill had achieved his goal of having a respectful dialogue with his daughter. He had completed what he believed was his moral duty to challenge what he saw as truly harmful notions in a way that his daughter could really hear him without shutting down, and he had preserved an authentic relationship with her where they could acknowledge their differences openly but peacefully. Bill's hope is that one day Sarah will look back on her "college rants" the way he now recalls his immature attitude toward commanding officers in his early days of the military. But regardless, Bill has met his goal of keeping a genuinely close, respectful, and authentic relationship with his daughter.

Conclusion

A Voice Worth Using

Throughout this book, we've explored myriad ways that language serves as a foundational pillar for mental health, social connection, and cognitive clarity. We've also examined the risks of self-censorship and the erosion of resilience when we treat disagreement as danger, and the unintended consequences of conflating words with violence. We've looked at clinical vignettes, academic research, and real-world stories that all point to one central truth: our capacity to speak freely—and to listen openly—is essential not only for a healthy society, but for a resilient mind.

The purpose of this book has not been to encourage everyone to always say everything on their minds. Rather, it has been to distinguish between judicious self-restraint and harmful self-censorship, and to provide tools for navigating that difference with integrity and confidence. The goal is not to win arguments, but to foster real understanding—of others, and of ourselves.

Free speech, like any freedom, carries responsibilities, but it also unlocks extraordinary benefits. It gives us the power to label and process our internal experiences, connect authentically with others, explore divergent viewpoints, and grow intellectually and emotionally. When we silence ourselves out of fear, we don't just protect others from discomfort—we cut ourselves off from the very tools we need to thrive.

Before we close, I'd like to share a personal reflection.

I grew up in Michigan, which at the time was a purple state. This meant I had friends and relatives who identified as blue, others who identified as red, and many who rejected labels altogether, choosing instead to evaluate each issue on its own merits. We would argue at the dinner table, in the workplace, even in the classroom or on the playground. And yet, none of the "Five Ds"—defriending, declining to date, disinviting, decreasing time, or dropping contact over politics—ever happened. That kind of reaction would have seemed extreme, and rather strange. Differences of opinion were expected and even valued. The point is, we were talking. We communicated. We sometimes got heated in the moment, but we always went out for the proverbial beer afterward (not on the playground, of course—there, we'd eventually just quit arguing and move on to double-Dutch jump rope).

I'll admit, my family might have been more interested in politics than the average family in our town. My grandmother, after all, was the first woman elected to our city council. But we weren't unique in having spirited opinions. There was a culture of caring about what was happening in our town, our state, and our country. We were able to talk about our differences, even (and especially) when we disagreed. My hope is that Americans, and people everywhere, can reclaim that spirit. Maybe part of what's gone wrong is that we've been told it's not polite to talk about politics to the point where we've forgotten how. Civility and silence are not the same thing; we can relearn how to disagree productively and even connect more deeply because of it. That we can speak our minds again without fear of cancellation.

The good news is that reclaiming your voice, or choosing to truly hear someone else as they reclaim theirs, is always an option. Whether you're an employee trying to navigate tricky workplace dynamics, a student wrestling with ideological conformity, or a family member wondering how to stay close without losing yourself, you now have tools to speak freely and listen resiliently. You've practiced how to reflect, plan, rehearse, and—when needed—choose not to engage, all with clarity and intention.

Open dialogue doesn't always lead to agreement. But when approached with candor and a willingness to listen, it leads to growth. It helps prevent the kinds of intellectual stagnation and emotional repression that can quietly erode our sense of self and our social fabric. And in a time when loneliness and anxiety are at record highs, authentic dialogue may be one of the most powerful medicines we have.

So, whether you're reading this because you've been silenced, because you're afraid of speaking, or because you've watched others suffer the consequences of saying the "wrong" thing, I hope this book has reminded you that your voice matters. And not only does it matter—it's worth cultivating, protecting, and using.

Speak freely. Listen deeply. Think clearly. Express your emotions authentically. And never forget: Words are not violence—they are vitality.

Appendix

Technique Worksheets

These worksheets are to help you apply the techniques from *Can I Say That? Why Free Speech Matters and How to Use It Fearlessly.* You don't need worksheets to do the techniques, but they are available to provide additional structure if needed. If you'd like to download additional copies, go to www.drchloe.com/freespeech.

SECTION 1: Building Awareness of Self-Censorship

Self-Censorship Check-In
1. Where do you tend to censor yourself?
   ❑ Home
   ❑ Work
   ❑ Social
   ❑ Other: _____

2. Why do you censor yourself?
   _____
   _____
   _____

3. List a few times you felt better after speaking openly. What did you discuss, and with whom? Why did it make you feel better?

   _____

   _____

   _____

   _____

4. List one time you felt worse after staying silent, and write down how you wish you had handled the situation. Remember that even when occasions have passed, it's still helpful to look back and understand how we could have done better. Even professional athletes watch video of past games to review what they could have done differently. This helps them to learn. If you feel stuck on how you could have handled the situation differently, ask someone you trust to help you brainstorm ideas.

   _____

   _____

   _____

   _____

5. Which of the four cognitive or five emotional gifts of language from the book do you most want to strengthen? In many cases, it's helpful to consciously decide to focus on these benefits. Check as many boxes as you wish. Think about these benefits when you feel tempted to self-censor.

   The Cognitive Gifts of Language:
   ❑ A Fundamental Process to Organize and Label Our Interior Life
   ❑ Enhancing Problem-Solving Abilities
   ❑ Build Metacognition and Insight
   ❑ Reduced Anxiety and Depression

The Emotional Gifts of Language:
- ❏ Regulating Emotional Responses
- ❏ Healthy Emotional Detachment and Insight
- ❏ Building Authentic Connections and Social Support
- ❏ Promoting Emotional Resilience
- ❏ Reducing Anxiety and Depression

6. Which of the Five Ds have you experienced or feared? Check as many boxes as applies, and write a bit about your responses to help build your awareness.
- ❏ Defriending
- ❏ Declining to date
- ❏ Disinviting
- ❏ Decreasing contact
- ❏ Dropping contact

_____

_____

_____

7. Identify any examples of topics where you think you might be overusing the defenses below to cover up important feelings or beliefs:

Suppression (Consciously choosing to stifle yourself):

_____

_____

_____

_____

Repression (Stifled yourself so habitually that you don't realize it as a conscious effort anymore, but you still recognize and connect with your views when you hear other people articulate them):

_____

_____

_____

_____

Denial (Being so disconnected from your true views that it's hard to admit or acknowledge them at this point, even if they are articulated clearly by others):

_____

_____

_____

_____

Now, do the opposite of suppression, repression, and denial. Go ahead and write down what you really think or feel about a situation you've been avoiding.

_____

_____

_____

_____

8. Which emotions do you associate with withholding your speech?
   - ❑ Anger
   - ❑ Numbness
   - ❑ Fear
   - ❑ Other: _____
   - ❑ Safety
   - ❑ Loneliness
   - ❑ Sadness

9. What emotions might arise if you spoke up more freely about things that matter to you?
   - ❑ Authenticity
   - ❑ Fear
   - ❑ Connectedness
   - ❑ Other: _____
   - ❑ Pride
   - ❑ Excitement

SECTION 2: Understanding Common Objections to Free Speech

1. Choose one common objection to free speech that makes you feel strongly. It can be a positive or negative reaction. Check the box by the objection that makes you feel the strongest. Once you've completed the follow-up questions about that objection, feel free to repeat the follow-up questions to explore your feelings about the other objections if you feel strongly about more than one objection.
   - ❏ What about hate speech and bullying? Isn't it better to create safe spaces?
   - ❏ What about the need for *some* limits on free speech?
   - ❏ What about misinformation?

2. Write your instinctual reaction to the objection:

   _____

   _____

   _____

   _____

3. Do you agree with your instinctual reaction? Are there others in your life who might not? Are there any points about the objections that you think would help for you, colleagues, or loved ones to reflect upon?

   _____

   _____

   _____

SECTION 3: Get Ready to Speak Up

1. Which of the tools will help you reduce self-censorship?
    ❑ Reflective Listening
    ❑ Make a Clear Plan for a Clear Head
    ❑ Role-play
    ❑ The WAIT Test
    ❑ Narrate Your Experience
    ❑ Take Ownership of Your Past Choice to Self-Censor
    ❑ Journal and Talk to Friends, or Mind-map

2. **WAIT Technique Planner**
Are you exploring the possibility of speaking up about something, but you want to make sure it's really the right thing to do? Do you want to make sure to proceed with caution? This worksheet will walk you through the WAIT technique step by step.

Want:
Are you sure you want to speak up about this? If so, why? If you're unsure or leaning toward staying quiet, what's giving you pause?

There are situations where speaking up is necessary—such as when you're heading toward marriage and your partner deserves to know about a significant financial issue. But in many other moments, whether to speak up is entirely up to you—like how much you choose to share about your personal values with colleagues or other parents at your child's track meet.

The goal is to speak up when it's important or meaningful to you, while also honoring your right to keep things private if that's what feels right. Take a moment and explore your thoughts or feelings on potentially speaking up about a particular topic:

_____

_____

_____

_____

Appropriate:

What would be the best time and place to have this conversation? What would be some times and places to avoid having this conversation?

_____

_____

_____

_____

Inoculate:

Sometimes, easing into a sensitive conversation helps build trust and gives you a chance to gauge how the other person might respond. For example, instead of launching into a detailed political opinion at a family gathering, you might start with a light comment or question to see how open others are to deeper discussion.

Inoculation is about sharing just enough to get a feel for the environment—so you can decide whether and how to go further. How could you "test the waters" by sharing a small piece of your perspective without diving all the way in?

_____

_____

_____

_____

Trust:

What's your trust level in this situation? How long have you known the people involved, and what has your relationship been like?

If you've had disagreements before, how were they handled? If confidentiality is a factor, how has that been respected in the past?

Also consider any power dynamics that may be present. For example, are you speaking to someone who has authority over you, like a professor or manager? Are there organizational policies that either support or restrict your ability to speak freely?

This step is about assessing whether the context—and the people in it—feel trustworthy enough for the conversation you're considering.

_____

_____

_____

_____

If you've worked through the WAIT steps and you do want to speak up, but you still feel anxious—rest assured, that's completely normal. Remember that the healthy function of anxiety is to stimulate preparation behaviors. You might find it helpful to explore the Clear Plan for a Clear Head techniques, which are designed to reduce anxiety by helping you prepare thoughtfully and speak with confidence. Taking additional preparation steps doesn't mean you *have* to speak up— it can simply be a way to explore what it feels like to move closer in that direction. Does a plan help increase your confidence? Or does formulating a potential plan help you realize that speaking up just doesn't feel right in this situation? If you tend to feel a lot of anxiety in general, you can also check out my previous book, *Nervous Energy: Harness the Power of Your Anxiety*.

3. Create a **clear plan for a clear head.**

   Describe a perplexing potential "speak up situation" in a couple of sentences. Include the outcome you'd like to achieve. For example, *"I am sick of sitting silently at extended family gatherings where everyone assumes I feel the same as they do, and makes derisive comments about people with my views. I'd like to peacefully share my perspective and then move on to other topics."*

   ❑ **Find an ally:** Having someone in your corner can make all the difference. Identify 2–3 people you could approach to share your plan to speak up, and let them know that their support would mean a lot.

   _____

   _____

   _____

   _____

   ❑ **Write your points down:** If you are worried about getting tripped up over your words or having a "brain freeze" during an important conversation, it can be helpful to write down your main points in advance. Write them down here, and then either take a copy with you to the conversation, make an acronym to keep them easy to recall during the conversation, or just trust yourself to remember them once you've taken the time to explore them on paper. Writing things down deepens our thought process and our sense of commitment to the material.

   _____

   _____

   _____

❑ **Say your line:** Sometimes, there's just one simple thing that needs to be said—yet, it feels overwhelmingly difficult to say. Is there one simple thing you need to stop overthinking, open your mouth, and simply say aloud to a particular person? If yes, you can write it down here and then simply deliver the line to that person when the time is right.

_____

_____

_____

_____

❑ **Consider your timing:** Would this conversation be best one to one? If yes, how can you ensure a calm, private conversation? Or, would it be best to have in front of others? Would it be helpful to give the person a heads-up that you want to talk, or just plan to respond differently next time they make certain predictable remarks? Set the stage for success.

_____

_____

_____

_____

❑ **Arm yourself with information:** Are there any facts you'd like to look up? Any handbooks you need to consult? Uncertainty increases anxiety, so empower yourself with knowledge if there's anything you think would help to clarify in advance.

_____

_____

_____

_____

❑ **Have a "debrief date" planned with someone supportive:**
List a few people who might be good options to connect
with after you speak up. To make it easy, remember that
you can get together in person or just by phone.

_____

_____

_____

_____

❑ **Thought replacements:** Write 2–5 thought replacements
that will help you stay focused and overcome feelings
of doubt (or overcome whatever feelings you predict
might sideline you or prevent you from fully expressing
yourself):

_____

_____

_____

_____

❑ **(Bonus Technique) Have a "pivot plan":** Pivot plans can
be helpful if you'd like to avoid dwelling on what you
know might be a topic of disagreement, but you still
want to make sure you express yourself. Your plan could
be to engage briefly about a topic just enough to make
your views known and hear anything the other person
wants to share, but then to shift the conversation onto
other topics that tend to be harmonious and interesting
for all. List a few good "pivot topics" you can raise when
you feel everyone has said their piece. Good examples are
often vacation plans, mutual hobbies, or shared projects
that you both enjoy.

_____

_____

_____

_____

4. **Self-reflection:** How did I feel preparing to speak? What
   helped?

   _____

   _____

   _____

   _____

   _____

   _____

SECTION 4: Learn to Listen Resiliently

Open dialogue isn't just about speaking your mind. It also includes
listening to others, even if we disagree.

1. What are your challenges about listening to others?
   - ❑ Fear of being taken by bad ideas
   - ❑ Fear of seeming like I agree with the speaker
   - ❑ Impatience to get my own point across
   - ❑ Frustration that someone I love could be so wrong (in
     my view)
   - ❑ Other: _____

2. What topics tend to test your patience when listening to others?
   - ❑ Abortion
   - ❑ Immigration
   - ❑ Gender and sexuality
   - ❑ Religion
   - ❑ Gun control
   - ❑ Voting for a certain
     party or candidate
   - ❑ Other: _____

3. Which techniques could help you to listen better?
   - ❑ "Find the Facts"
   - ❑ Relax Your Body—and Your Mouth!
   - ❑ Imagine an Audience:

4. Who is someone that, if they were watching your conversation, you'd want them to see you as a good and respectful listener? Think of that person (or people) when you are struggling to remain respectful or you feel tempted to interrupt. List a few potential people to imagine when an audience might inspire your best listening skills:

   _____

   _____

   _____

5. Count the Minutes, Count the Questions, and Transfer the Grace
   What's your goal for how many minutes you can listen, or how many questions you can ask, before jumping in to respond?

   _____

   _____

   _____

6. What are a couple of memories from your past where you held a viewpoint that now seems silly at best, for which you can now give yourself a grace that you can extend to others as well?

   _____

   _____

   _____

7. Thought Replacements
   What are some thought replacements that would help you
   to listen better?

   _____

   _____

   _____

   _____

   _____

SECTION 5: Putting It All Together

1. Which vignette felt closest to home for you? What lessons
   or ideas for action can you take from it? Even beyond the
   vignettes, what are some themes, ideas, or techniques you've
   learned that you'd like to carry onward in your life? Check
   the boxes next to the vignettes that resonated the most for
   you, and then write about your takeaways below.

   ❑ **Vignette: My Personal Last Straw**
   *Dr. Chloe's experience of "coming out of the closet" on her true
   views about masking children, and its connection to overall
   awareness about the mental health benefits of free speech.*

   ❑ **Vignette: Calista and the Secondary Gains of
   Victimhood**
   *Calista overcomes an attachment to the victim role in the
   workplace, and thereby confronts issues directly so she can
   develop new skills that help her succeed.*

   ❑ **Vignette: Courtney's Fear of Words**
   *Courtney gets exposed to new information that makes her
   think differently than she believes the entirety of her friend
   group thinks—and she actually discovers a few kindred
   spirits after she finds the courage to share openly.*

❏ **Vignette on the Dangers of Groupthink**
   A couple struggles to stand up to a bevy of doctors regarding their daughter's medical treatment.

❏ **Vignette: Olivia Finds Her Voice**
   Olivia finds her authentic voice to express herself to an aunt who assumes that Oliva agrees with her on everything.

❏ **Vignette: Mark Reconnects with Himself**
   Mark reconnects with parts of himself he had buried in order to get along at the office.

❏ **Vignette: Andrew Learns to Listen**
   Andrew initially thinks he must "go no contact" with his sister, but discovers they can actually coexist in peace.

❏ **Vignette: Bill and Sarah Play the Long Game**
   Bill works on nonjudgmental listening while staying true to himself in order to preserve his relationship with his daughter.

2. Lessons or ideas for action:

_____

_____

_____

_____

_____

Thank you so much for exploring these worksheets! Feel free to share with me about how you're applying or expanding what you've learned. You can reach me at www.drchloe.com/freespeech, where you can also learn more about book clubs or other activities around this book.

If this book has sparked any insights or helped you find your voice, I'd love to hear about it. Whether you've applied one of the tools, adapted a technique in your own way, or created a new one

entirely, your experience matters. I also welcome you to stay connected—whether by inviting me to speak to your group, attending one of my workshops, or bringing this book into your book
club—I'm happy to join virtually for a discussion. We learn best
through thoughtful exchanges, and I'd be honored to be part of
those conversations. Please connect on social media or visit me at
www.drchloe.com/FreeSpeech to stay in touch.

Acknowledgments

The privilege of writing this book has been an incredible gift. I'm deeply grateful to my mentor, Dave Kerpen, for encouraging me to pursue it and for facilitating the introductions that helped bring it to life. I also thank my editor, Michael Campbell, for the opportunity to partner with Skyhorse and for his thoughtful input that challenged and supported me throughout the process.

My heartfelt thanks to my friend and colleague Judith Zackson, who has encouraged me to speak my mind ever since our days in graduate school. Thanks also to my therapist and coach Ana Tucker, for encouraging me to take bold steps forward (ironically, there was a time when I was afraid to speak up and write this book!). Also, thanks to my amazing assistant, Donna Dayanan—this would not have been possible without you!

To my husband, Jim—thank you for your unwavering support and countless behind-the-scenes contributions that made this journey possible.

This book is dedicated to my son, William. I was fortunate to grow up in an America where speaking your mind felt natural, not dangerous. I want him to have that same privilege: to grow up unafraid to speak the truth, and to see differing views as a sign of freedom, not a source of fear.

About the Author

Dr. Chloe Carmichael is a clinical psychologist and *USA Today* bestselling author known for helping high-functioning individuals express themselves with clarity and confidence. She holds a doctorate in clinical psychology from Long Island University and a BA from Columbia University, where she graduated summa cum laude and was elected to Phi Beta Kappa.

Her previous book, *Nervous Energy: Harness the Power of Your Anxiety*, was endorsed by Deepak Chopra. It features practical tools to access the healthy function of anxiety, which is to stimulate preparation behaviors. The book has been used by leaders in business, law, and the creative arts to channel anxiety into productivity.

Dr. Carmichael's work has been featured by a wide range of media, including *Fox News, NewsNation, ABC Nightline*, and *Inside Edition*. She frequently speaks to audiences at universities, law firms, nonprofits, and private groups. She also enjoys connecting with readers through virtual or in-person book clubs.

To invite Dr. Carmichael to speak to your group or organization, visit DrChloe.com for more information.

Notes

Introduction

1 The Editorial Board, "America Has a Free Speech Problem," *The New York Times*, March 18, 2022, https://www.nytimes.com/2022/03/18/opinion/cancel-culture-free-speech-poll.html.

2 Google, "Be Authentic," Google Trends, accessed May 15, 2025, https://trends.google.com/trends/explore?q=be%20authentic&geo=US&date=all.

3 Jeffrey M. Jones, "More U.S. College Students Say Campus Climate Deters Speech," *Gallup*, March 12, 2018, https://news.gallup.com/poll/229085/college-students-say-campus-climate-deters-speech.aspx.

4 Thomas F. Pettigrew and Linda R. Tropp, "A Meta-Analytic Test of Intergroup Contact Theory," *Journal of Personality and Social Psychology* 90, no. 5 (2006): 751–783, https://doi.org/10.1037/0022-3514.90.5.751.

5 Jesse Morton, "A Former al-Qaeda Recruiter Speaks," *Clearer Thinking with Spencer Greenberg*, May 5, 2022, https://podcast.clearerthinking.org/episode/103/jesse-morton-a-former-al-qaeda-recruiter-speaks/.

6 John Villasenor, "Views among College Students Regarding the First Amendment: Results from a New Survey," *Brookings Institution*, September 18, 2017, https://www.brookings.edu/articles/views-among-college-students-regarding-the-first-amendment-results-from-a-new-survey/.

7 Greg Lukianoff and Rikki Schlott, *The Canceling of the American Mind: How Cancel Culture Undermines Trust, Destroys Institutions, and Threatens Us All* (New York: Simon & Schuster, 2023), 84.

8 Scott Jaschik, "New Analysis: New England Colleges Responsible for Left-Leaning Professoriate," *Inside Higher Ed*, July 5, 2016, https://www.insidehighered.com/news/2016/07/05/new-analysis-new-england-colleges-responsible-left-leaning-professoriate.

9 Stanley Rothman, S. Robert Lichter, and Neil Nevitte, "Politics and Professional Advancement among College Faculty," *The Forum* 3, no. 1 (2005), https://doi.org/10.2202/1540-8884.1067.

10 Mitchell Langbert, Anthony J. Quain, and Daniel B. Klein, "Faculty Voter Registration in Economics, History, Journalism, Law, and Psychology,"

Econ Journal Watch 13, no. 3 (2016): 422–51, https://econjwatch.org/articles /faculty-voter-registration-in-economics-history-journalism-communications -law-and-psychology.

11 Ronnie Janoff-Bulman and Nate C. Carnes, "Social Justice and Social Order: Binding Moralities across the Political Spectrum," *PLoS ONE* 11, no. 3 (2016): e0152479, https://doi.org/10.1371/journal.pone.0152479.

12 April Bleske-Rechek, Eric Giordano, Eric Kasper, Geoffrey Peterson, and Timothy Shiell, UW System Student Views on Freedom of Speech: Summary of Survey Responses (University of Wisconsin System, February 1, 2023), https://www.wisconsin.edu/civil-dialogue/download/SurveyReport 20230201.pdf.

13 Orly Eitan, Domenico Viganola, Yoel Inbar, Anna Dreber, Magnus Johannesson, Thomas Pfeiffer, Stefan Thau, and Eric Luis Uhlmann, "Is Research in Social Psychology Politically Biased? Systematic Empirical Tests and a Forecasting Survey to Address the Controversy," *Journal of Experimental Social Psychology* 79 (November 2018): 188–99, https://doi .org/10.1016/j.jesp.2018.06.004.

14 Amy Mitchell, Jeffrey Gottfried, Jocelyn Kiley, and Katerina Eva Matsa, *Political Polarization & Media Habits* (Pew Research Center, 2014), https: //www.pewresearch.org/journalism/2014/10/21/political-polarization-media -habits/.

15 Daniel A. Cox, *The State of American Friendship: Change, Challenges, and Loss* (Washington, DC: Survey Center on American Life, 2021), https://www .americansurveycenter.org/research/the-state-of-american-friendship -change-challenges-and-loss/.

16 Anna Brown, "Most Democrats Who Are Looking for a Relationship Would Not Consider Dating a Trump Voter," *Pew Research Center*, April 24, 2020, https://www.pewresearch.org/short-reads/2020/04/24/most-democrats -who-are-looking-for-a-relationship-would-not-consider-dating-a-trump -voter/.

17 Gallup and Knight Foundation, *Free Expression on Campus: What College Students Think About First Amendment Issues* (Washington, DC: Gallup, Inc., 2017), https://knightfoundation.org/wp-content/uploads/2020 /01/Knight_Foundation_Free_Expression_on_Campus_2017.pdf.

18 Public Religion Research Institute, *Analyzing the 2024 Presidential Vote: PRRI's Post-Election Survey*, December 13, 2024, https://www.prri.org /research/analyzing-the-2024-presidential-vote-prris-post-election-survey/.

19 Eric Lendrum, "Study: Democrats More Likely to Cut Off Relatives Over Political Differences," *American Greatness*, December 23, 2024, https: //amgreatness.com/2024/12/23/study-democrats-more-likely-to-cut-off -relatives-over-political-differences/.

20 Samuel J. Abrams, "Polarization in American Family Life is Overblown," *Survey Center on American Life*, February 23, 2022, https://www.american surveycenter.org/polarization-in-american-family-life-is-overblown/.

21 Public Religion Research Institute, *Dueling Realities: Amid Multiple Crises, Trump and Biden Supporters See Different Priorities and Futures for the Nation* (Washington, DC: PRRI, 2020), https://www.prri.org/research /amid-multiple-crises-trump-and-biden-supporters-see-different-realities -and-futures-for-the-nation/.

Chapter 1: The Cognitive Gifts of Language

1   Naomi I. Eisenberger, Shelley E. Taylor, Shelly L. Gable, Clayton J. Hilmert, and Matthew D. Lieberman, "Neural Pathways Link Social Support to Attenuated Neuroendocrine Stress Responses," *NeuroImage* 35, no. 4 (2007): 1601–12, https://doi.org/10.1016/j.neuroimage.2007.01.038.
2   Tobias Grossmann, Regine Oberecker, Stefan Paul Koch, and Angela D. Friederici, "The Developmental Origins of Voice Processing in the Human Brain," *Neuron* 65, no. 6 (2010): 852–58, https://uvababylab.org/wp-content /uploads/2016/04/21-22-page/Grossmann-et-al.-Neuron-2010.pdf.
3   Annekatrin Wetzstein and Winfried Hacker, "Reflective Verbalization Improves Solutions—The Effects of Question-Based Reflection in Design Problem Solving," *Applied Cognitive Psychology* 18, no. 2 (2004): 145–56, https://doi.org/10.1002/acp.949.
4   Leif Stinessen, "The Influence of Verbalization on Problem-Solving," *Scandinavian Journal of Psychology* 26, no. 1 (1985): 342–47, https://doi.org /10.1111/j.1467-9450.1985.tb01173.x.
5   John R. Hayes, *The Complete Problem Solver*, 2nd ed. (Hillsdale, NJ: Lawrence Erlbaum Associates, 1989).
6   F. R. Ruud Van der Weel and Audrey L. H. Van der Meer, "Handwriting but Not Typewriting Leads to Widespread Brain Connectivity: A High-Density EEG Study with Implications for the Classroom," *Frontiers in Psychology* 14 (2023): 1219945, https://doi.org/10.3389/fpsyg.2023.1219945.
7   Benjamin Franklin effect: Jecker & Landy, 1969: Asking some-one for a small favor can make them more favorable towards you. Jecker, Jon, and David Landy. 1969. *"Liking a Person as a Function of Doing Him a Favor." Human Relations* 22 (4): 371–78. https://doi.org /10.1177/001872676902200407. Pratfall effect: Aronson, 1966: Needing small favors makes highly competent people seem more likeable. Aronson, Elliot. 1966. *"The Effect of a Pratfall on Increasing Interpersonal Attractiveness." Psychonomic Science* 4 (6): 227–28. https://doi.org/10.3758 /BF03342263.
8   Jeffrey E. Young, *Cognitive Therapy for Personality Disorders: A Schema-Focused Approach* (Sarasota, FL: Professional Resource Exchange, 1989), https://archive.org/details/cognitivetherapy0000youn.
9   Aaron T. Beck, *Depression: Clinical, Experimental, and Theoretical Aspects* (New York: Harper & Row, 1967).
10 Carmichael, Chloe. 2021. *Nervous Energy: Harness the Power of Your Anxiety*. New York: St. Martin's Press.

11 Robert I. Levy, *Tahitians: Mind and Experience in the Society Islands*, rev. ed. (Chicago: University of Chicago Press, 1975).

12 Gary Lupyan, David H. Rakison, and James L. McClelland, "Language Is Not Just for Talking: Redundant Labels Facilitate Learning of Novel Categories," *Psychological Science* 18, no. 12 (2007): 1077–83, https://doi .org/10.1111/j.1467-9280.2007.02028.x.

13 Langbert, Quain, and Klein, "Faculty Voter Registration."

Chapter 2: The Emotional Gifts of Language

1 Margaret S. Clark and Eli J. Finkel, "Does Expressing Emotion Promote Well-Being? It Depends on Relationship Context," in *The Social Life of Emotions*, ed. Larissa Z. Tiedens and Colin Wayne Leach (Cambridge: Cambridge University Press, 2004), 106, https://www.google.com/books /edition/The_Social_Life_of_Emotions/t-5GiBys-dkC?hl=en&gbpv=0.

2 D. W. Winnicott, *The Maturational Processes and the Facilitating Environment: Studies in the Theory of Emotional Development* (London: Hogarth Press and the Institute of Psycho-Analysis, 1965), https://selfdefinition.org/burns /DW-Winnicott-The-Maturational-Process-and-the-Facilitating-Environment -1965.pdf.

3 Wilfred R. Bion, *Learning from Experience* (London: Heinemann, 1962), accessed May 13, 2025, https://pep-web.org/search/document/ZBK.003.0000A ?page=PR0004.

4 Laura Sels, Anh Tran, Katharine H. Greenaway, Lesley Verhofstadt, and Elise K. Kalokerinos, "The Social Functions of Positive Emotions," *Current Opinion in Behavioral Sciences* 39 (2021): 41–45, https://doi.org/10.1016/j .cobeha.2020.12.009.

5 Susan Folkman, "The Case for Positive Emotions in the Stress Process," *Anxiety, Stress & Coping* 21, no. 1 (2008): 3–14, https://doi.org/10.1080 /10615800701740457.

6 The *DSM* (*Diagnostic and Statistical Manual of Mental Disorders*) is the primary classification system used by mental health professionals in the United States to diagnose psychiatric conditions. It is published by the American Psychiatric Association.

7 Noam Chomsky, *Aspects of the Theory of Syntax* (Cambridge, MA: MIT Press, 1965), https://archive.org/details/aspectsoftheoryo00chom.

8 Noam Chomsky, *New Horizons in the Study of Language and Mind* (Cambridge: Cambridge University Press, 2000).

9 Steven Pinker, *The Language Instinct: How the Mind Creates Language*, reprint ed. (New York: Harper Perennial Modern Classics, 2007).

10 Peter G. Enticott, Patrick J. Johnston, Sally E. Herring, Kate E. Hoy, and Paul B. Fitzgerald. 2008. "Mirror Neuron Activation Is Associated with Facial Emotion Processing." *Neuropsychologia* 46 (11): 2851–2854. https: //doi.org/10.1016/j.neuropsychologia.2008.04.022.

11 Yichuan Liu, Elise A. Piazza, Erez Simony, Patricia A. Shewokis, Banu Onaral, Uri Hasson, and Hasan Ayaz, "Measuring Speaker-Listener Neural

Coupling with Functional near Infrared Spectroscopy," *Scientific Reports* 7 (2017): 43293, https://doi.org/10.1038/srep43293.

12 Karim S. Kassam, Amanda R. Markey, Vladimir L. Cherkassky, George Loewenstein, and Marcel Adam Just, "Identifying Emotions on the Basis of Neural Activation," *PLOS ONE* 8, no. 6 (2013): e66032, https://doi.org/10.1371/journal.pone.0066032.

13 Eisenberger et al., "Neural Pathways."

14 D. A. Misch, "Basic Strategies of Dynamic Supportive Therapy," *The Journal of Psychotherapy Practice and Research* 9, no. 4 (2000): 173–89.

15 John Bowlby, "The Nature of the Child's Tie to His Mother," *The International Journal of Psycho-Analysis* 39, no. 5 (1958): 350–73.

16 Lei Zheng, Qian Lu, and Yiqun Gan, "Effects of Expressive Writing and Use of Cognitive Words on Meaning Making and Post-Traumatic Growth," *Journal of Pacific Rim Psychology* 13 (January 2019): e5, https://doi.org/10.1017/prp.2018.31.

17 Antonella Trotta, Andrew J. Gerber, Felicitas Rost, Sarah Robertson, Avi Shmueli, and Rosine J. Perelberg, "The Efficacy of Psychodynamic Psychotherapy for Young Adults: A Systematic Review and Meta-Analysis," *Frontiers in Psychology* 15 (2024): 1366032, https://doi.org/10.3389/fpsyg.2024.1366032.

18 Stefan G. Hofmann, Anu Asnaani, Imke J. J. Vonk, Alice T. Sawyer, and Angela Fang, "The Efficacy of Cognitive Behavioral Therapy: A Review of Meta-Analyses," *Cognitive Therapy and Research* 36, no. 5 (2012): 427–40, https://doi.org/10.1007/s10608-012-9476-1.

Chapter 3: The Hidden Dangers of Self-Censorship

1 The word "politics" derives from Greek *politikos*, from *politēs* 'citizen,' from *polis* 'city.' It literally just means, "citizens of the city."

2 A study at the University of Wisconsin found that 41 percent of students had refrained from expressing their viewpoint in class because they feared it would hurt their grade. Bleske-Rechek et al., UW System Student Views.

3 Ceyhun Ersan, "Early Language Development and Child Aggression," *World Journal of Education* 10, no. 1 (2020): 1–11, https://doi.org/10.5430/wje.v10n1p1.

4 Alejandra Suarez, Dug Y. Lee, Christopher Rowe, Alex Anthony Gomez, Elise Murowchick, and Patricia L. Linn, "Freedom Project: Nonviolent Communication and Mindfulness Training in Prison," *SAGE Open* 4, no. 1 (2014): 1–12, https://doi.org/10.1177/2158244013516154.

5 Sonja P. Brubacher, Martine B. Powell, Krystal Lockwood, Susan Dennison, Tara Renae McGee, and Janet Ransley, "The Importance of Enhancing the Communication Skills of Incarcerated Mothers," *Aggression and Violent Behavior* 70 (2023): 101825, https://doi.org/10.1016/j.avb.2023.101825.

6   Bayarbaatar Puntsagsuren, "Recidivists Rehabilitation Through Interpersonal Interaction," *Russian Journal of Deviant Behavior* 4, no. 1 (2024): 85–92, https://doi.org/10.35750/2713-0622-2024-1-85-92.

7   Thomas Abt, Mark Mills, and Grace Magori, *Cognitive Behavioral Interventions: Scaling Success to Save Lives* (College Park: Center for the Study and Practice of Violence Reduction, University of Maryland, 2025), https://vrc.umd.edu/sites/vrc.umd.edu/files/2025-03/VRC_CBI%20White%20Paper_FINAL_3.19.25-compressed_1.pdf.

8   Ryan Rifai, "KKK Members Leave Klan after Befriending Black Musician," Al Jazeera, January 9, 2017, https://www.aljazeera.com/features/2017/1/9/kkk-members-leave-klan-after-befriending-black-musician.

9   Elizabeth Chervonsky and Caroline Hunt, "Suppression and Expression of Emotion in Social and Interpersonal Outcomes: A Meta-Analysis," *Emotion* 17, no. 4 (2017): 669–83, https://doi.org/10.1037/emo0000270.

10 Maximilian Scheuplein and Anne-Laura van Harmelen, "The Importance of Friendships in Reducing Brain Responses to Stress in Adolescents Exposed to Childhood Adversity: A Preregistered Systematic Review," *Current Opinion in Psychology* 45 (June 2022): 101310, https://doi.org/10.1016/j.copsyc.2022.101310.

11 Pinker, *The Language Instinct.*

12 Greg Lukianoff and Jonathan Haidt, *The Coddling of the American Mind: How Good Intentions and Bad Ideas Are Setting Up a Generation for Failure*, Illustrated ed. (New York: Penguin Books, 2019).

13 Naomi Isenberg and Markus Brauer, "Commitment and Consistency," in *Routledge Encyclopedia of Psychology*, 2022, https://doi.org/10.4324/9780367198459-REPRW126-1.

14 Nader Hajloo, "Relationships between Self-Efficacy, Self-Esteem and Procrastination in Undergraduate Psychology Students," *Iranian Journal of Psychiatry and Behavioral Sciences* 8, no. 3 (2014): 42–49.

15 John Lane, Andrew M. Lane, and Anna Kyprianou, "Self-Efficacy, Self-Esteem and Their Impact on Academic Performance," *Social Behavior and Personality* 32, no. 3 (2004): 247–56, https://doi.org/10.2224/sbp.2004.32.3.247.

16 Christina Tran, *Self-Efficacy's Mediating Role on the Relationship Between Personality and Depression in the Unemployed* (master's thesis, San José State University, 2024), https://doi.org/10.31979/etd.gmg9-ykt5.

17 Jason Thompson and Rapson Gomez, "The Role of Self-Esteem and Self-Efficacy in Moderating the Effect of Workplace Stress on Depression, Anxiety and Stress," *Australasian Journal of Organisational Psychology* 7 (2014), https://doi.org/10.1017/orp.2014.2.

18 P. K. Maciejewski, H. G. Prigerson, and C. M. Mazure, "Self-Efficacy as a Mediator between Stressful Life Events and Depressive Symptoms: Differences Based on History of Prior Depression," *The British Journal of Psychiatry* 176 (April 2000): 373–78, https://doi.org/10.1192/bjp.176.4.373.

19 Richard A. Griggs, *Psychology: A Concise Introduction* (United Kingdom: Worth Publishers, 2008).

20 House Judiciary Committee GOP, "Mark Zuckerberg just admitted three things: 1. Biden-Harris Admin 'pressured' Facebook to censor Americans . . .," *Facebook*, April 29, 2024, https://www.facebook.com/share/p/1EfXQ7K dRM/.

21 U.S. House of Representatives, Committee on the Judiciary, and Select Subcommittee on the Weaponization of the Federal Government, *The Censorship-Industrial Complex: How Top Biden White House Officials Coerced Big Tech to Censor Americans, True Information, and Critics of the Biden Administration*, Interim staff report, May 1, 2024. https://judiciary.house .gov/sites/evo-subsites/republicans-judiciary.house.gov/files/evo-media -document/Biden-WH-Censorship-Report-final.pdf.

22 Brian Flood, "Elon Musk Gives Dave Rubin Behind-the-Scenes Look at Twitter and What Causes Shadowbans," *Fox News*, December 12, 2022, https://www.foxnews.com/media/elon-musk-gives-dave-rubin-behind-scenes -look-twitter-shadowbans.

23 Greg Wehner, "Elon Musk Invites Blacklisted Stanford Professor to Twitter Headquarters," *New York Post*, December 12, 2022, https://nypost .com/2022/12/12/elon-musk-invites-blacklisted-stanford-professor-dr -jay-bhattacharya-to-twitter-headquarters/.

24 NORC at the University of Chicago. n.d. "Get the Data." *General Social Survey*. Accessed May 13, 2025. https://gss.norc.org/us/en/gss/get-the -data.html.

25 Sam Peltzman, *The Socio Political Demography of Happiness*, New Working Paper Series No. 331 (Chicago: University of Chicago Booth School of Business, Stigler Center for the Study of the Economy and the State, 2023), https://hdl.handle.net/10419/274143.

26 Barry R. Schlenker, John R. Chambers, and Bonnie M. Le, "Conservatives Are Happier Than Liberals, but Why? Political Ideology, Personality, and Life Satisfaction," *Journal of Research in Personality* 46, no. 2 (2012): 127– 46, https://doi.org/10.1016/j.jrp.2011.12.009.

27 Van Hiel, Alain, and Lieven Brebels. 2011. "Conservatism Is Good for You: Cultural Conservatism Protects Self-Esteem in Older Adults." *Personality and Individual Differences* 50 (1): 120–123. https://doi.org/10.1016/j.paid .2010.09.011.

28 Catherine Gimbrone, Lisa M. Bates, Seth J. Prins, and Katherine M. Keyes, "The Politics of Depression: Diverging Trends in Internalizing Symptoms among US Adolescents by Political Beliefs," *SSM—Mental Health* 2 (December 2022), https://doi.org/10.1016/j.ssmmh.2021.100043.

Chapter 4: Three Common Objections to Free Speech

1 Christopher F. Rufo, "Quotations from Chairman Maher," *City Journal*, April 17, 2024, https://www.city-journal.org/article/quotations-from-chairman-maher.

2   National Review, "John Kerry Says the First Amendment Is Getting in the Way of Online Censorship," *National Review*, October 1, 2024, https://www.nationalreview.com/news/john-kerry-says-the-first-amendment-is-getting-in-the-way-of-online-censorship/.

3   Freedom Forum, *Where America Stands: The First Amendment 2024 Report* (Washington, D.C.: Freedom Forum, 2024), https://www.freedomforum.org/content/uploads/2024/11/Freedom-Forum-Where-America-Stands-Report-2024-4.pdf.

4   Joshua Q. Nelson, "University Rescinds Reprimand for Professor Who Failed Student for Using Term 'Biological Woman,'" *New York Post*, July 8, 2023, https://nypost.com/2023/07/08/university-rescinds-reprimand-for-professor-who-failed-student-for-using-term-biological-woman/.

5   New York Times Co. v. Sullivan, 376 U.S. 254 (1964), https://tile.loc.gov/storage-services/service/ll/usrep/usrep376/usrep376254/usrep376254.pdf.

6   Google Trends for words are violence—United States, 2004—present ee Interest over time-Google, *Google Trends: "words are violence,"* accessed May 13, 2025, https://trends.google.com/trends/explore/TIMESERIES/1740480000?hl=en-US&tz=300&date=all&geo=US&q=words+are+violence&sni=3.

7   David Hudson, "80 Years Ago the Supreme Court Introduced 'Fighting Words,'" *FIRE (Foundation for Individual Rights and Expression)*, March 9, 2022, https://www.thefire.org/news/80-years-ago-supreme-court-introduced-fighting-words.

8   Jack Greiner, "'Red Headed Bitch' Not Fighting Words," *Faruki PLL Blog*, July 14, 2023, https://www.ficlaw.com/blog/red-headed-bitch-not-fighting-words.

9   *R.A.V. v. City of St. Paul*, 505 U.S. 377 (1992), https://www.supremecourt.gov/opinions/boundvolumes/505bv.pdf.

10   For example, Michale Conklin and Nadine Strossen Michael Conklin, "Anti-Semitism and The Overlooked Benefits of Allowing 'Hate Speech,'" *Indiana Journal of Law and Social Equality* 11, no. 1 (2023): 197–207, https://www.repository.law.indiana.edu/ijlse/vol11/iss1/7/.

11   Lily FitzGibbon, Cansu Ogulmus, Greta M. Fastrich, Johnny King L. Lau, Sumeyye, Lorella Lepore, and Kou Murayama, "Understanding the Forbidden Fruit Effect: People's Desire to See What Is Forbidden and Unavailable," *OSF Preprints*, preprint, 2020, https://osf.io/preprints/osf/ndpwt_v1.

12   European Commission, *Report on the Implementation of EU Anti-Racism Action Plan 2020–2025 and on National Action Plans Against Racism and Discrimination*, COM(2024) 419 final (Brussels: European Commission, 2024), https://commission.europa.eu.

13   Nicholas Kristof, "'How Can You Hate Me When You Don't Even Know Me?'" *New York Times (Online)*, June 26, 2021, https://www.proquest.com/blogs-podcasts-websites/how-can-you-hate-me-when-don-t-even-know/docview/2545265441/se-2.

14 *Cohen v. California*, 403 U.S. 15 (1971), https://tile.loc.gov/storage-services /service/ll/usrep/usrep403/usrep403015/usrep403015.pdf.

15 *Roe v. Wade*, 410 U.S. 113 (1973), https://tile.loc.gov/storage-services/service /ll/usrep/usrep410/usrep410113/usrep410113.pdf.

16 U.S. Department of Health and Human Services, *Protecting Youth Mental Health: The U.S. Surgeon General's Advisory* (Washington, DC: U.S. Department of Health and Human Services, 2021), https://www.hhs.gov/sites /default/files/surgeon-general-youth-mental-health-advisory.pdf.

17 National Center for Education Statistics, *2022 NAEP Mathematics Assessment: Highlighted Results at Grades 4 and 8 for the Nation, States, and Districts* (Washington, DC: U.S. Department of Education, 2022), https: //www.nationsreportcard.gov/highlights/mathematics/2022/

18 Hilary Cass, *Independent Review of Gender Identity Services for Children and Young People: Final Report* (London: NHS England, 2024), https: //webarchive.nationalarchives.gov.uk/ukgwa/20250310143933/https://cass .independent-review.uk/home/publications/final-report/.

19 Socialstyrelsen (The National Board of Health and Welfare), *Care of Children and Adolescents with Gender Dysphoria: Summary of National Guidelines* (Stockholm: Socialstyrelsen, 2022), https://www.socialstyrelsen.se/globalassets /sharepoint-dokument/artikelkatalog/kunskapsstod/2023-1-8330.pdf.

20 Finland's COHERE recommends that medical treatment for gender dysphoria be given only after thorough psychosocial support and evaluation. Hormonal or surgical interventions are approved case-by-case, based on lasting distress, functional impairment, and psychological readiness. Non-medically necessary or cosmetic procedures are excluded, and more research is encouraged on outcomes and regrets. COHERE Finland, *Summary of a Recommendation by COHERE: Medical Treatments for Gender Dysphoria That Reduces Functional Capacity in Transgender People—Recommendation* (Helsinki: Council for Choices in Health Care in Finland, 2020), https: //palveluvalikoima.fi/documents/1237350/22895838/Summary +transgender.pdf/2cc3f053-2e34-39ce-4e21-becd685b3044/Summary +transgender.pdf?t=1592318543000.

21 Patient safety for children and adolescents with gender incongruence. Ukom (Norwegian Commission of Inquiry), *Pasientsikkerhet for barn og unge med kjønnsinkongruens [Patient Safety for Children and Adolescents with Gender Incongruence]* (Stavanger: Ukom, 2023), https://ukom.no /rapporter/pasientsikkerhet-for-barn-og-unge-med-kjonnsinkongruens /sammendrag.

22 NHS England, "Children and Young People's Gender Services: Implementing the Cass Review Recommendations," last updated August 29, 2024, https://www.england.nhs.uk/long-read/children-and-young-peoples-gender -services-implementing-the-cass-review-recommendations/.

23 American Society of Plastic Surgeons (ASPS) statement to press regarding gender surgery for adolescents.

American Society of Plastic Surgeons, "ASPS Statement to Press Regarding Gender Surgery for Adolescents," *PSN Extra*, August 14, 2024, https://www.plasticsurgery.org/for-medical-professionals/publications /psn-extra/news/asps-statement-to-press-regarding-gender-surgery-for -adolescents.

24 The American Society of Plastic Surgeons becomes the first major medical association to challenge the consensus of medical groups over "gender -affirming care" for minors. Leor Sapir, "A Consensus No Longer," *City Journal*, August 12, 2024, https://www.city-journal.org/article/a-consensus -no-longer.

Part Two: Tools for Open Dialogue

1 A 2017 Gallup and Knight Foundation poll found that 65 percent of college students believe their campus climate discourages free speech, and a 2022 Knight poll found that less than half of college students feel their free speech rights are secure. Jones, "Campus Climate Deters Speech."

2 The Halo Effect is a textbook psychological term to describe the lasting tendency of first impressions. Edward L. Thorndike, "A Constant Error in Psychological Ratings," *Journal of Applied Psychology* 4, no. 1 (1920): 25–29, https://psycnet.apa.org/record/1920-10104-014.

Chapter 5: Seven Tools for Speaking Up

1 James P. Morris, Nancy K. Squires, Charles S. Taber, and Milton Lodge, "Activation of Political Attitudes: A Psychophysiological Examination of the Hot Cognition Hypothesis," *Political Psychology* 24, no. 4 (December 2003): 727–45, https://doi.org/10.1046/j.1467-9221.2003.00349.x.

2 Joanne V. Wood, W. Q. Elaine Perunovic, and John W. Lee, "Positive Self-Statements: Power for Some, Peril for Others," *Psychological Science* 20, no. 7 (July 2009): 860–66, https://doi.org/10.1111/j.1467-9280.2009.02370.x.

3 Irwin Altman and Dalmas A. Taylor, *Social Penetration: The Development of Interpersonal Relationships* (New York: Holt, Rinehart & Winston, 1973), https://archive.org/details/socialpenetratio00altm.

4 Nancy L. Collins and Lynn Carol Miller, "Self-Disclosure and Liking: A Meta-Analytic Review," *Psychological Bulletin* 116, no. 3 (1994): 457–75, https://doi.org/10.1037/0033-2909.116.3.457.

5 Wenzhen Li, Zhiya Zhao, Dajie Chen, Mei-Po Kwan, and Lap Ah Tse, "Association of Health Locus of Control with Anxiety and Depression and Mediating Roles of Health Risk Behaviors among College Students," *Scientific Reports* 15, no. 1 (2025): 7565, https://www.nature.com/articles /s41598-025-91522-x.

6 Aaron Lazare, *On Apology* (New York: Oxford University Press, 2004), https://www.amazon.com/Apology-Aaron-Lazare/dp/0195173430.

Chapter 6: Five Tools for Self-Restraint

1 ". . . you had people that were very fine people on both sides . . . and I'm not talking about the neo-Nazis and the white nationalists, because they should be condemned totally—but you had many people in that group other than neo-Nazis and white nationalists . . ." POLITICO Staff, "Trump's Comments on White Supremacists, 'Alt-Left' in Charlottesville," *Politico*, August 15, 2017, https://www.politico.com/story/2017/08/15/full-text-trump-comments-white-supremacists-alt-left-transcript-241662.

2 Raymond S. Nickerson, "Confirmation Bias: A Ubiquitous Phenomenon in Many Guises," *Review of General Psychology 2*, no. 2 (1998): 175–220, https://journals.sagepub.com/doi/10.1037/1089-2680.2.2.175.

3 John M. Gottman and Nan Silver, *The Seven Principles for Making Marriage Work* (New York: Harmony Books, 2015).

4 Kenny Xu, *An Inconvenient Minority: The Attack on Asian American Excellence and the Fight for Meritocracy* (New York: Center Street, 2021), https://www.amazon.com/Inconvenient-Minority-Admissions-American-Excellence/dp/1635767563.

5 Xu, *An Inconvenient Minority*.

6 Melissa Bateson, Daniel Nettle, and Gilbert Roberts, "Cues of Being Watched Enhance Cooperation in a Real-World Setting," *Biology Letters* 2, no. 3 (2006): 412–14, https://doi.org/10.1098/rsbl.2006.0509.

7 For example, a person who angrily insists that sexism is the root of wage disparities between men and women, and refuses to consider the fact that women work shorter hours overall even in the context of "full time employment." John Phelan, "Harvard Study: 'Gender Wage Gap' Explained Entirely by Work Choices of Men and Women," *Foundation for Economic Education*, December 10, 2018, https://fee.org/articles/harvard-study-gender-pay-gap-explained-entirely-by-work-choices-of-men-and-women/.

8 Hiroaki Kawamichi, Kazufumi Yoshihara, Akihiro T. Sasaki, Sho K. Sugawara, Hiroki C. Tanabe, Ryoji Shinohara, Yuka Sugisawa, and Norihiro Sadato, "Perceiving Active Listening Activates the Reward System and Improves the Impression of Relevant Experiences," *Social Neuroscience* 10, no. 1 (2015): 16–26, https://www.tandfonline.com/doi/full/10.1080/17470919.2014.954732.

Index

201